NOW YOU'RE COOKING!

To all the kids who have cooked with us – past, present and future – we want you to know that the possibilities in the kitchen are endless. It's not just about the food; it's about the conversations, the confidence and the magic of making a good day even better with a good meal.

You've got this – we believe in you. Now you're cooking!

Jolene and Lily Mae x

NOW YOU'RE COOKING!

70 RECIPES THAT KIDS CAN MAKE

Jolene and Lily Mae Cox

NINE BEAN ROWS

CONTENTS

INTRODUCTION	3
BEGIN WITH THE BASICS	4
KITCHEN KIT	12
PREP SKILLS FOR BEGINNERS	14
KNIFE SKILLS FOR LEVEL-UPPERS	20
KEEP IT CLEAN	24
KITCHEN RULES	26
THE CLASSICS	28
BREAKFAST AND BRUNCH	50
LOVE YOUR LUNCHBOX	72
AFTER-SCHOOL FUEL	94
TRAY BAKES AND ONE-POT WONDERS	116
EPIC EATS	138
SWEET TREATS	160
INDEX	182
ACKNOWLEDGEMENTS	186

INTRODUCTION

I'm Lils and I'm 11. I've been cooking with my mum ever since she could sit me up in a feeding chair.

My mum is Jolene. Her mission is to teach kids how to cook real food we love to eat, using proper ingredients and having fun doing it.

This cookbook isn't like most other kids' cookbooks. It's a real cookbook for real kids like me and you, not just another book full of food that grown-ups think we'd want to make. I've flipped through other kids' cookbooks and found recipes for stuffed aubergines or bulgur wheat salad. Want to get a kid excited about cooking? Make sure they actually want to eat the food!

Yes, lots of our recipes include veggies, but hear me out: we couldn't make a totally beige cookbook (and we know you wouldn't want that either). The veggies we use are the ones you probably already know and like, and honestly, they taste great in these dishes.

Here's a fun fact: did you know your taste-buds grow and change over time? It's true! And here's a secret: my mum used to hate veggies when she was a kid, but now she loves them. So even if you don't like them now, give them a try and you might start to. But if not, no big deal – just leave them out for now. The main thing is that you'll be cooking with fresh ingredients and the key is to keep trying.

My mum always says (she talks a lot, my mum), 'The biggest lessons in life come when things don't go as planned – it's the mistakes that help us grow and learn.' And she's right. Everyone has burned toast at least once, even top chefs.

Cooking is something you can do at any age, and with the right tips and tricks, you'll only get better with practice. Remember, we all have to start somewhere. So whether you're boiling an egg for the first time or ready to level up your knife skills, now you're cooking!

BEGIN WITH THE BASICS

Learning the basics will help you to understand what you're doing, which will give you more confidence in the kitchen. With these skills, you'll be able to cook safely, have fun and create delicious meals. The more you cook, the more these skills will become second nature.

HOW TO PREHEAT THE OVEN

Preheating the oven means letting it warm up so that it's hot when you put the food inside. This is very important when you're cooking. The food will start to cook as soon as it goes in the oven, so set a timer and do other little jobs (like cleaning up messy countertops) while you wait for it to preheat. A fan oven usually takes about 10 minutes to reach 180°C.

To preheat the oven, turn it on.

If you have a fan-assisted oven, set it to the fan mode. All the recipes in this book have been tested using a fan oven.

If you're using a conventional oven (in other words, one without a fan), use the temperature that's 20°C higher than the temperature given for a fan oven. The temperature is higher because the hot air doesn't move around in a conventional oven as well without a fan.

No matter which kind of oven you're using, set it to the temperature given in the recipe. Wait for the oven to tell you it's ready before you put the food inside. Some ovens have a light that will turn off when it has reached the temperature you set it to.

HOW TO WEIGH INGREDIENTS

Measuring ingredients accurately is super important, especially for baking. Baking is like a science – it needs to be exact.

To use a digital scale, press the power button and wait for the screen to show the number 0. Most scales can switch between grams and ounces. Our recipes use grams, so press the unit button until you see the letter g on the display.

If you're weighing something like flour or sugar, you need to put it in a bowl, but the bowl adds extra weight. To get around this, put the empty bowl on the scale and press the tare button to reset the scale to zero. Now you will only be measuring the ingredient, not the bowl.

Slowly add your ingredient to the bowl or put it directly on the scale. Stop when you reach the amount you need for your recipe.

HOW TO LINE BAKING TRAYS AND TINS

Lining baking trays with non-stick baking paper stops food from sticking to the tray and makes it easier to clean up. All our recipes call for non-stick baking paper, which isn't always the same thing as parchment paper or greaseproof paper, so read the label on the box carefully. Trust me, you don't want to be peeling paper off the bottom of the food you worked so hard to make!

To line a flat baking tray, grab a roll of non-stick baking paper. Measure it against the tray, then cut it with scissors so it's the same size.

Here's a trick to help the paper lay flat: scrunch the paper into a ball, then smooth it out. It will now fit on the tray better and won't curl up at the edges.

If the paper still moves around, rub a little butter or oil on the tray first, then put the paper on it. This helps the paper to stick and stay in place.

To line a square or rectangular baking tin, put it on top of the non-stick baking paper. Cut a piece that's big enough to cover the bottom and sides, with extra hanging over the edges too.

Cut a small slit at each corner of the paper. This helps the paper fold neatly inside the tin.

If you want, you can grease the tin with a little butter or oil to help the paper stick and stay in place.

Now put the paper inside the tin. Press it down so it fits nicely. The extra paper hanging over the sides will make it easy to lift your baked treat out of the tin later.

HOW TO MAKE MUFFIN LINERS

You can make your own tulip muffin liners like the ones you see in a bakery using non-stick baking paper.

1 Cut out 12 x 15cm squares of non-stick baking paper.

2 Cut small slits about 5cm deep on each corner. It will look like a flower with four petals.

3 Use a pastry brush to paint the bottom of each hole in your muffin tin with a little oil. This will help the liners to stick in them. Put a paper square into each hole. Use a small cup to push it down into place.

4 The edges of the liner will fold in on themselves, but that's okay.

Pour your muffin batter into the lined cups. The paper might pop up a little, but that's fine, it will go down when baking. If it pops up too much, though, cut the slits a little deeper next time.

HOW TO CRACK AN EGG

Grab a small bowl to crack the egg into. This helps to catch any little pieces of shell that might fall in before you add the egg to your recipe.

Hold the egg in one hand and tap it on the edge of the bowl or on the countertop. Tap softly until you see a little crack. Now use both thumbs to pull the shell apart over the bowl and let the egg slide out.

If any pieces of shell fall in, which is bound to happen sometimes, the best way to scoop them out is to use the eggshell itself. If you try to use a spoon or your fingers, it's much trickier to get.

HOW TO SEASON FOOD WITH SALT AND PEPPER

Seasoning your food (which is kitchen-speak for adding salt and pepper) makes it taste better. This is because salt dials up the flavour for your taste-buds. Adding the right amount of salt shouldn't make your food taste salty, just more delicious.

The golden rule of seasoning is to start with a little bit. You can always add more, but you can't take it out once it's in!

To add a pinch of salt, pour a little into the palm of your hand. Use your fingers and thumb to take a small pinch and sprinkle it on your food. We like to put our salt in a salt pig (like the one in this photo!) or a small bowl to make it easy to grab pinches out of.

Do the same thing with ground pepper if you're using it. Or if you have a pepper grinder, turn it over your food. A couple of twists is usually enough.

Another pro trick to seasoning your food is to scatter over the salt and pepper from a height. This means holding your hand or pepper grinder high above the food as you sprinkle the salt or pepper over it. Doing it this way means the seasoning gets added more evenly across the food, not all in one place.

HOW TO USE A BLENDER

Never use a blender when you're alone in the kitchen – always ask an adult for help.

Before you touch the blender (or any electrical equipment), make sure your hands are dry. If your hands are wet, electricity can travel through the water and give you a shock, which can be dangerous.

When adding food to a blender, always keep the blender unplugged and keep your hands away from the blades. The blades are very sharp to cut the food, so they can cut you too! If you need to push food down, use a wooden spoon or a spatula, never your fingers.

When everything is inside, put the lid on tightly so nothing splashes out. Plug in the blender and turn it on to a low speed, then increase the speed if needed.

When you're done, turn off the blender and unplug it. We're all about doing things yourself, but this is one time when you should ask an adult to clean it.

HOW TO USE A HOB

Be careful around the hob. Pay attention to where you put your hands, as the hob gets very hot and can burn you.

Keep tea towels and oven mitts away from the hob too. If they get too close to a hot ring, they can burn or even catch on fire.

Always turn the handles of pots and pans in towards the hob – never let them hang over the edge of the hob.

Keep small children and pets away from the hob.

The heat level depends on the level of the flame if you're using a gas hob or the number it's set to if you're using an electric hob. A low heat is when the flame or dial is turned to a low setting, a medium heat is when the flame or dial is midway and a high heat is the highest setting.

Always remember to turn the hob off when you have finished cooking.

HOW TO DRAIN HOT WATER SAFELY

A lot of food needs to be boiled, so you need to know how to drain the hot water safely.

Put a colander in the sink. Using both hands, pick up the handle of the saucepan and bring it over to the sink. Slowly and carefully pour the contents of the pan into the colander. Let the water pour off first before you tip the pan to empty the food into the colander.

If you're using a big pot of water, it will be heavy, so put an empty, medium-sized saucepan or bowl next to the large pot. Use tongs, a large slotted spoon or a kitchen spider to carefully scoop the food into the empty pan or bowl, then ask an adult to empty the pot.

Be careful of the steam when you're draining food. Hot steam can burn just as badly as boiling water.

HOW TO TAKE HOT FOOD OUT OF THE OVEN

Before you open the oven door, put your oven gloves on. Never touch a hot tray, tin or dish with your bare hands!

When you open the oven door, stand back because hot steam will come out.

When the steam has disappeared, use both hands to hold the baking tray, tin or dish firmly and lift it out carefully. Put it on a heatproof surface, like a wooden chopping board or on top of the hob, so it doesn't burn your countertops.

When you're done, close the oven door and turn it off.

Always be careful around hot trays and dishes that have just come out of the oven. I leave the oven gloves next to the hot dish as a reminder not to grab it with my bare hands.

HOW TO TEST THAT CHICKEN IS COOKED

Chicken must be cooked all the way through so that it's safe to eat – eating undercooked chicken can make you sick.

To check that chicken is cooked, cut into the thickest part of the chicken. If the inside is all white with no pink, it's ready to eat. But if you see any pink, it needs more time to cook. If it's still pink, put it back in the oven or pan and check it again in a few minutes.

If you have a digital thermometer, put it in the thickest part of the chicken. When the temperature reaches 73.8°C (165°F), it's safe to eat.

Remember, if there's no pink in sight, only pure white, then it's cooked just right!

KITCHEN KIT

PREP SKILLS FOR BEGINNERS

Anyone can get into the kitchen and start cooking, no matter what age you are. But we love to think outside the box for first-timers and have come up with easy, safe ways to prep all kinds of food.

On pages 20–23, we show you how to use a knife safely with some of our tried-and-tested tips and tricks. But if you want to build up your confidence first, we have lots of other ways to tackle kitchen tasks without using knives just yet. Each technique has been designed with safety in mind while still giving you that feeling of accomplishment and independence.

HOW TO PEEL AND GRATE GARLIC

Pull a garlic clove from the bulb. Put the clove on a chopping board and press down on it with the flat side of a butter knife. The skin will crack, making it easy to peel off.

Hold a handheld grater steady over a plate or bowl, then rub the garlic against the grater in one direction. Keep your fingers away from the sharp edges. The garlic will turn into a paste as you grate it, so use a butter knife to scrape it off the grater. Stop when the garlic gets too small to hold safely.

Or try this: Just start grating the unpeeled clove. The papery skin will naturally peel away and protect your fingers at the same time.

HOW TO PEEL AND GRATE GINGER

To peel ginger, use the edge of a small spoon to gently scrape off the thin skin. A spoon works better than a peeler because it removes just the skin without wasting too much of the ginger.

Hold a handheld grater steady over a plate or bowl, then rub the ginger against the grater in one direction. Keep your fingers away from the sharp edges. The ginger will turn into a paste as you grate it, so use a butter knife to scrape it off the grater. Stop when the ginger gets too small to hold safely.

Or try this: Peel thumb-sized pieces of fresh ginger, then pop them into a freezerproof bag. Grate however much you need straight from the frozen ginger, then put the rest back in the bag. It's actually easier to grate frozen ginger because it isn't as tough as it is when it's fresh. The grated frozen ginger will be like snow.

A GRATE TIP

You can grate lots of garlic and ginger in advance and freeze them in 1 teaspoon portions in a silicone ice cube tray. When they're frozen solid, pop them out of the tray and store them in a freezerproof bag or container for up to three months, ready to add straight to the recipe.

HOW TO GRATE CHEESE

Use a box grater because the handle makes it easy to hold it steady, and the larger holes make it easier to grate a lot. I love lifting up the grater to reveal a large mound of cheese, like a sandcastle.

Put the box grater on a flat surface, like a chopping board, and hold it steady with one hand. Choose the right side of the grater depending on whether you want big or small shreds. Hold the cheese at the top and press it firmly against the grater. Move the cheese down the grater, then lift it back up and repeat. Keep your fingers away from the sharp holes to stay safe. Stop grating when the cheese gets too small to hold safely. Great grating!

HOW TO CHOP AN ONION

Onion goggles at the ready – this might get emotional!

Peel off the onion skin.

Push a fork firmly into the top of the onion and hold the handle with your non-writing hand. Using your writing hand, peel off thin layers of the onion with a vegetable peeler, moving the onion around in a circle as you go.

When you've peeled enough, use your kitchen scissors to cut the larger chunks into smaller pieces.

ONION GOGGLES

Have you ever wondered why onions sometimes make you cry when you cut them? It's self-defence! They are releasing a substance that stings our eyes to try to stop us from eating them. We've tried countless ways to stop the tears, from holding a spoon in our mouths to eating chocolate to distract ourselves. But the only thing that truly works is onion goggles (or any goggles). Plus they make cooking more fun.

HOW TO PREPARE SPRING ONIONS

Hold the spring onions together over a bowl. Use clean kitchen scissors to snip the green tops into small pieces, letting them fall straight into the bowl. Make sure your fingers stay away from the scissor blades and take slow, careful snips.

A lot of the kids in our cooking classes say that the white part of the spring onion tastes too strong, so you can save the white parts for another time. But if you do like them, you can snip them into small pieces using the scissors too.

HOW TO MAKE CARROT RIBBONS

Carrot ribbons are a great way to add carrots to a dish if you're not ready to use a knife yet.

Scrub the carrots and peel them with a vegetable peeler. Throw away or compost the outer peelings.

Now just keep using the peeler to shave off thin strips, peeling until you get to the hard core in the middle. Flip the carrot over and peel ribbons off the other side too.

If you need smaller ribbons, use your scissors to slice or cut them into matchsticks. When you're ready to level up and use a knife, use the methods on pages 22–23.

HOW TO SLICE OR DICE PEPPERS

Hold the pepper in both hands and use your thumbs to firmly press the stalk down into the middle. It should loosen and become wobbly. Pull the stalk out in one quick motion. Turn the pepper over and shake it to remove all the seeds.

Use your kitchen scissors to cut the pepper in half. Cut off any white parts, which are bitter, then cut each half into strips. If you want diced peppers, just snip each strip into smaller pieces.

HOW TO PEEL AND GRATE AN APPLE

Use a vegetable peeler to remove the outer layer of skin.

Hold the apple and grate it using the large holes on a box grater set on top of a plate or chopping board. Rotate the apple as you grate it, stopping when you reach the core in the middle.

HOW TO CHOP FRESH HERBS

Hold a small bunch of herbs by their stems over a bowl. Using clean kitchen scissors, carefully snip the herbs into small pieces, letting them fall into the bowl. Keep your fingers away from the blades and take slow, gentle snips. If you want finer pieces, put your scissors in the bowl and continue snipping until they are as small as you like.

To cut basil or mint into nice thin strips, stack a few leaves on top of each other, then roll them up tightly into a little tube, like a sleeping bag. Hold the roll steady and use scissors to cut across it, creating thin ribbons.

HOW TO ZEST CITRUS FRUIT

Hold a handheld grater steady over a bowl or chopping board with one hand. With your other hand, press the citrus fruit firmly against the grater and move it back and forth. Rotate the fruit as you go, making sure to only grate the outer colourful layer. Don't grate the white part underneath the skin, as it's too bitter.

HOW TO SLICE A CHICKEN FILLET

Before and after touching raw chicken, scrub your hands with soap and warm water.

Keep your hands away from your face, eyes and mouth while handling chicken. You're on a mission to stay clean.

Chicken needs its own VIP section, so keep it on its own special chopping board – no mingling with raw veggies or any other foods allowed. If you're using colour-coded chopping boards, remember that the red one is for raw meat (read page 24 for more on this).

Put the chicken on your clean chopping board. Hold it steady with one hand or you can use a fork to keep your fingers extra safe.

Use kitchen scissors to snip the chicken into strips or bite-sized pieces. Start at one end and work your way across. Go slowly and carefully, making sure you keep your fingers away from the scissor blades. If the pieces are too big, just snip them smaller.

When you're done with the chicken, scrub the chopping board, scissors, countertops and your hands with warm soapy water.

KNIFE SKILLS FOR LEVEL-UPPERS

Once you've mastered the beginner skills, you're ready to level up and unlock the next stage.

SAFETY TIPS FOR KNIVES

Keep your board steady. Put a clean damp cloth under the chopping board to stop it from slipping.

Choose the right knife. Pick a small, sharp knife that feels comfortable in your hand. It shouldn't be too large or heavy – make sure it's right for the job.

Sharp knives are safer. A sharp knife is actually safer than a dull one because it cuts through food easily and with more control.

Never run with knives. If you need to move around the kitchen with a knife, keep it pointed down and held at your side, just like you would with scissors.

No licking knives. It might be tempting, but knives are never for licking! Keep them far away from your mouth.

HOW TO CLEAN A SHARP KNIFE SAFELY

Wash it separately. Always wash your knife right after you use it. Never leave it in the sink, where it might get hidden under dishes.

Use warm soapy water. Hold the knife by the handle. Use a sponge or dishcloth to carefully wipe the blade from the back of the knife towards the edge. Never rub along the sharp side.

Be careful with the blade. Keep your fingers away from the sharp edge while washing. Clean the knife from the base of the blade to the tip in smooth motions.

Rinse and dry immediately. After washing, rinse the knife with clean water and dry it right away with a clean towel, holding the handle and wiping away from the sharp edge.

Store safely. When the knife is clean and dry, store it in a knife block, on a magnetic knife strip or in a drawer with a cover.

A NOTE FOR THE ADULTS

Try to resist the urge to take over. It's all about finding a balance between being careful and letting us kids develop a lifelong skill. If you keep taking over and interrupting, we'll lose our confidence and won't enjoy the experience. So take a step back, offer encouragement and trust us. As long as the safety tips are followed, everyone stays safe and we learn something new. A little praise and positive direction go a long way here!

THE BRIDGE METHOD

The bridge method (or Lego hand, as I also like to call it) is perfect for cutting round foods like onions, carrots, potatoes and apples in half. Cutting them in half first means they won't roll around, which makes cutting safer. This method also keeps your fingers safe and gives you more control while cutting.

Hold the knife in your writing hand.

With your other hand, put your thumb on one side of the food and a finger on the other side, forming a 'bridge' over the food.

Put the knife under the bridge, keeping your other fingers out of the way. This makes sure no fingers are near the blade.

Now carefully cut the food in half.

THE CLAW METHOD

The claw method is great for chopping fruit and vegetables into smaller pieces while keeping your fingers safely tucked in. Make sure you're only using this method on pieces of food that are flat on the board (like half an onion) that you've already cut in half using the bridge method.

Hold the knife in your writing hand.

Create a closed 'claw' shape with the fingers of your other hand, tucking your fingertips in. Use this claw to hold the food in place on the board.

As you chop, move your claw hand further back, keeping it out of the knife's reach.

KNIFE SKILLS FOR LEVEL-UPPERS

THE SCATTER METHOD

When you've chopped your food using the claw method, it's time to finish with the scatter method to even out the pieces or chop them into smaller pieces.

Spread your chopped pieces of food evenly across the chopping board.

Hold the knife in your writing hand, with the blade pointing down towards the board.

Put the fingers of your other hand on the blunt side of the knife to help guide it.

Gently guide the knife downwards, chopping the pieces of food into smaller, more even sizes.

THE MEZZALUNA METHOD

A mezzaluna is a great tool to use to chop safely when you're just starting out. It's a curved, two-handled knife that lets you chop things easily – and the best part is that your fingers never get near the blade.

To use a mezzaluna, put your chopped fruit, vegetables or herbs on a chopping board. Hold both handles firmly with your hands and rock the blade back and forth over the ingredients. Keep moving the mezzaluna across the board to make sure everything is evenly chopped.

KEEP IT CLEAN

I totally get it – cleaning is the worst. But there's a good reason why you have to keep it clean in the kitchen, and it's not just because adults love to say 'because I said so'. It's because if you don't clean up properly, you can get sick. I don't know about you, but I hate being sick way more than I hate cleaning. So keep it clean and avoid the icky stuff.

WASH YOUR HANDS

If you're like me and spend most of your life upside-down in a handstand, it's important to keep your hands clean, especially when you're about to cook up a storm.

- Wash your hands with warm water and antibacterial soap.
- Rub between your fingers, thumbs and all parts of your hands for at least 20 seconds. Don't forget your fingernails. My mum always says you could plant spuds under mine, so give them a good scrub with a nail brush.
- Rinse well with water and dry with a clean towel.

START AND FINISH WITH A CLEAN WORK SURFACE AND FLOOR

Wipe your surfaces with a clean cloth and warm soapy water before you start cooking and when you're done.

As for the floor, sweep up any crumbs and toss them in the bin. (Or you could open the door and let the dog hoover them up ... just kidding!)

CLEAN UTENSILS

Imagine me saying this in my best action-hero voice: 'Using knives comes with great responsibility.' Clean your cooking utensils with warm soapy water, taking extra care when handling sharp knives. Read page 20 for more tips on how to clean your knives safely.

CHOPPING BOARDS

It's a good idea to have at least two chopping boards – one for raw meat and one for vegetables – because you never want to prepare fresh foods on a board that you've already used for raw meat.

Coloured chopping boards are an even better way to avoid cross-contamination. Big word, I know, but you never want germs from raw food getting into ready-to-eat food, and using colour-coded chopping boards helps with this. In all professional kitchens, the colours are:

- Red for raw meat
- Blue for raw fish
- Yellow for cooked meat
- Green for salad and fruit
- Brown for vegetables
- White for bakery and dairy
- Purple for allergens and free-from foods.

WOODEN CHOPPING BOARDS

It's a good idea to have a wooden chopping board so that you can put hot trays, tins and dishes on it when they come out of the oven to protect your countertop. Don't use a plastic chopping board for this, it could melt.

To clean a wooden chopping board, cut a lemon in half and sprinkle it with salt (no, this isn't the start of a recipe!). Add a few drops of washing-up liquid and a little water, then use the lemon as a scrubber. The combination of lemon, salt and soap will create a magical foam. Now scrub, scrub, scrub! When you're done, rinse the board with warm water and let it drip dry.

KITCHEN RULES

Never cook alone. Always make sure there's an adult nearby when you're ready to work your magic in the kitchen. They're your back-up, so keep them in the loop before you get started.

Follow the instructions on page 20 every time you use a knife. Safety first, chef!

Read the recipe – twice! But seriously, always read the recipe before you start to cook to get a feel for it before diving in. Trust me, it makes everything easier.

Get your gear ready. Set out all the equipment you need before you start to cook so you're not scrambling to find it midway through the recipe.

Measure, prepare and chop all your ingredients before you start to cook. Put them all in separate bowls and line them up like TV chefs do. Put everything in order, just like they do on cooking shows. You'll feel like a total pro.

Ask for help when you need it. You can rock every recipe in this book, but don't be afraid to ask for help, especially with taking hot food out of the oven or draining hot water (read page 10 again).

Be extra careful around the hob. Always keep saucepan handles turned in so that they aren't hanging over the side of the hob, which could cause an accident.

When you're cooking, just cook. No sneakily watching your tablet in between steps.

Don't wear headphones or ear buds while cooking. But background music? Absolutely! Play your favourite tunes on a speaker to keep the vibes going.

Go at your own pace and don't rush.

Have fun – now you're cooking!

CLAS

THE
SSICS

PERFECT BOILED WHITE RICE

Rice is one of the most popular foods on the planet – it's a staple for more than half of the world's population. Yet many adults are still trying to master the art of cooking it. We use the 2-to-1 ratio method, which gives you perfectly cooked, fluffy rice every time.

Serves 2

1 cup long-grain white rice or basmati rice

2 cups water

½ teaspoon salt

1. You can use any cup or mug, but you have to measure the rice and water with the same cup or mug to get the ratio right. So start by measuring 1 cup of rice and putting it in a large bowl.

2. Now you're going to rinse the rice to remove extra starch, which means the rice won't get too sticky. Cover the rice in the bowl with cold water, then swirl it around gently with your fingers.

3. Put a colander in the sink, then put a fine mesh sieve on top of the colander. Carefully drain off the water by pouring it into the fine mesh sieve.

4. Put the rice back in the bowl, cover it with cold water, swirl it and drain it again. Repeat these steps two or three more times, until the water that drains off is clear.

5. Put the rice in a medium-sized saucepan. Using the same cup or mug that you used to measure the rice, pour 2 cups of water into the saucepan. Add the salt.

6. Put the saucepan on a high heat on the hob. When the water starts to boil, stir the rice with a wooden spoon and turn the heat down to low, then cover the saucepan with a lid.

7. Let the rice cook on a low heat for 15 minutes. Don't lift the lid while it cooks. I know how tempting it can be, but just leave it alone to let the steam work its magic.

8. After 15 minutes, check if the rice is cooked by carefully lifting the lid (watch out for the escaping steam). Take a little rice with a fork, blow on it so it's not too hot, and try it. Perfectly cooked rice should be firm but tender, so if it's still too hard, put the lid back on and let it cook for 5 more minutes.

9. When the rice is cooked, turn off the heat. Keep the lid on the pan and let it sit for 5 minutes.

10 Remove the lid, again being careful of the steam that will come out when you take the lid off. Use a fork to fluff up the rice, gently breaking up any clumps. Using a fork instead of a spoon keeps the grains separate and fluffy.

11 Your perfectly cooked rice is now ready to serve.

CRACKING GOOD EGG-FRIED RICE

To make a cracking good egg-fried rice, you need to start with cold, cooked rice. Leftover rice is perfect, but there are a few rules to remember.

You must store leftover rice safely, because if it's left out too long in a warm kitchen, harmful bacteria can grow on it and eating it could make you sick. The key is to cool it down as quickly as possible, so spread your cooked rice out on a baking tray or in a large baking dish in a thin, even layer. Put the tray or dish in the fridge, uncovered, for about 20 minutes, until the rice is cold. Scoop the rice into an airtight container, pop the lid on and store it in the fridge. Use leftover rice within two days.

Serves 2

1 garlic clove

2 spring onions or 4 fresh chives

2 large eggs

2 tablespoons sesame oil

100g frozen peas

400g cold, cooked white rice (page 30)

1 tablespoon soy sauce

salt and pepper

1. This recipe takes only a few minutes to make, so the trick is to prepare and weigh all your ingredients and have everything ready to go in separate small bowls first.

2. Peel and grate the garlic. Use clean kitchen scissors to snip the green tops of the spring onions or the chives into small pieces. Crack the eggs into a small bowl, then whisk them with a fork.

3. Put the sesame oil in a non-stick frying pan, then put the pan on a medium heat on the hob and let the oil warm up.

4. Add the grated garlic and frozen peas to the hot pan. Stir them with a wooden spoon for 1 minute, until your peas turn bright green.

5. Add the cold, cooked rice. Stir it gently to break up any clumps and cook for 2 minutes to heat it up.

6. Push the rice and peas to the sides of the pan, making a clear circle in the middle. Pour the beaten eggs into the centre and let them cook for about 1 minute, stirring as they turn from liquid to solid. When they're nicely scrambled, mix the eggs into the rice.

7. Add the soy sauce and a little salt and pepper, then stir everything together.

8. To serve, divide between two bowls. Time to eat!

PERFECT MASHED POTATOES

There are lots of different types of potatoes, and each one works best for different cooking methods. To make the perfect mash, you need a floury potato. At first, I thought that meant flower-shaped potatoes, but nope, I couldn't find any of those in the bag. A floury potato is one that is high in starch. Maris Piper potatoes are good for mash because they have lots of starch, which makes your mash fluffy and smooth. They can also soak up lots of butter and milk, giving your mash that dreamy, creamy texture.

Perfect mashed potatoes are a plate of happiness. Some adults even judge how good a restaurant is based on its mash. But like all simple classics, when it goes wrong, it goes really wrong. Did you know you can't fix lumpy mashed potatoes with an electric hand mixer? It only makes the mash worse, turning it into a gloopy, lumpy mess. (My mum says we all need a little kitchen disaster to learn from now and again, and she has learned this one the hard way!) But don't worry, we're sharing the simple secrets to perfect mash. From this day forward, you can make restaurant-quality mashed potatoes every time.

Serves 4

1.2kg Maris Piper potatoes

50g unsalted butter

50ml cream (single or double)

salt and pepper

1. Peel the potatoes using a peeler, then cut them into even-sized chunks. This makes sure they all cook at the same rate.

2. Put the potato chunks in a large saucepan and add just enough cold water to cover them. Don't overfill the pan – about one-third of the pan should remain clear of water so it doesn't boil over. If your saucepan is too small, switch to a bigger one.

3. Put the saucepan on a high heat on the hob and bring the water to a boil, no lid needed. When the water starts boiling, let it keep boiling and set a timer for 15 minutes.

4. After 15 minutes, check if the potatoes are done by lifting out a few chunks with a slotted spoon. Put them on a clean chopping board and poke them with a fork. If the fork slides in easily all the way through, they're ready. If it doesn't, cook them for 5 more minutes and check again.

5. When the potatoes are cooked, turn off the heat. Put a colander in the sink and drain the potatoes (read the tips on page 10 for how to drain hot water safely).

6   Let the spuds sit in the colander for a minute to make sure all the water has drained off – this helps prevent watery mash.

7   Put the potatoes back in the saucepan and let them dry out in the heat of the saucepan for a minute or two. This extra step makes fluffier mash.

8   Add the butter and let it melt into the potatoes.

9   Move the saucepan onto a clean tea towel or a wooden chopping board. Grab your potato masher and, using both hands if needed, mash the potatoes, breaking them up completely by pushing the masher through the potatoes over and over again. Keep mashing until they're smooth.

10 Pour half of the cream into the potatoes while mashing, adding just enough to get the perfect creamy texture – you might not need all the cream. Remember, you can always add more but you can't take it out if you add too much.

11 Finally, add a little salt and pepper, give it all one more stir and enjoy your perfect mashed potatoes.

OVEN-BAKED GNOCCHI

Got leftover mashed potatoes? Turn them into homemade gnocchi! Gnocchi (pronounced NYOCK-ee) are little potato dumplings from Italy. The trick to making them light and fluffy is not overloading them with flour, which makes them dense and heavy. Start with a little flour and gradually add more to make lovely potato pillows.

Traditionally gnocchi are boiled, but baking them in the oven makes them golden brown and crispy on the outside and fluffy on the inside. Who knew leftovers could be this good?

Serves 4

1 egg

500g leftover mashed potatoes (page 34)

100g to 150g plain flour, plus extra for the countertop

1 teaspoon salt

1 tablespoon olive oil

To serve:

classic tomato sauce (page 46), arrabbiata sauce (page 48), pesto rosso (page 82) or melted butter and grated Parmesan

1. Preheat your oven to 200°C for a conventional oven or 180°C for a fan oven.

2. Line a baking tray with non-stick baking paper.

3. Crack your egg into a large mixing bowl, then use a fork to whisk it up.

4. Add the mashed potatoes, flour and salt. Use a wooden spoon to gently mix it all together. You want it to turn into a soft, slightly sticky dough that holds together without crumbling. You can use your hands to mix it, but don't overwork it. Add a little more flour only if needed until you get the right consistency. Remember, you can always add more flour but you can't take it out!

5. If the dough feels too sticky, sprinkle in up to 50 grams more flour, but don't go overboard. If it's too dry, a splash of olive oil will help to bring it together.

6. Sprinkle your chopping board with a little flour. Tip the dough out onto the chopping board and roll it into a large sausage shape, then cut it into bite-sized pieces with a butter knife.

7. You don't have to do this part, but it makes your gnocchi look fancy and helps the sauce to stick to them. Sprinkle 1 or 2 tablespoons of flour onto a fork and your gnocchi to prevent sticking. Put the fork on the countertop, with the prongs facing down and slightly tilted. Working with one at a time, press one piece of gnocchi against the fork with your thumb, then roll it down to create ridges.

8. Put the gnocchi on the lined baking tray and spread them out in a single layer. Pour the olive oil into a small bowl, then use a pastry brush to paint the tops of all the gnocchi with oil.

9. Put the tray in the preheated oven and cook for 30 minutes, until the gnocchi are golden brown and getting crispy on the edges.

10 Use oven gloves to carefully remove the tray from the oven and put it on a wooden chopping board or on the hob. Your gnocchi are now ready to serve with a simple tomato sauce, arrabbiata sauce, pesto rosso or even just a little melted butter and grated Parmesan cheese.

CRISPY-SKIN BAKED POTATOES

Just like the perfect mash, the best baked potatoes start with choosing the right kind of potato. Maris Piper potatoes are floury potatoes. They turn light and fluffy on the inside and crispy on the outside, making the perfect baked potato. They also make great mash and chips. Rooster potatoes are a good all-rounder spud. They turn golden and tasty when roasted and baked. No matter which kind of potato you use, this recipe will give you the fluffiest insides and crispiest outsides of any baked potato you've ever put a fork in.

Makes 4

4 medium Maris Piper or Rooster potatoes

2 tablespoons olive oil

salt and pepper

1. Preheat your oven to 200°C for a conventional oven or 180°C for a fan oven.

2. Line a baking tray with non-stick baking paper.

3. Scrub the potatoes under cold running water to remove any dirt. Pat them dry with a clean tea towel, then use a fork to poke several holes in each potato. This helps steam escape while they bake so they don't explode (exploding potatoes are never a good thing!).

4. Put the potatoes on the lined baking tray. Drizzle some of the oil on each potato, then use your hands to rub the oil all over them. This will help make the skins crispy. Sprinkle a little salt and pepper over each potato.

5. Put the tray in the preheated oven and bake for 50 minutes. After 50 minutes, use oven gloves to carefully remove the tray from the oven and put it on a wooden chopping board or on the hob to protect your countertop.

6. Poke each potato with a butter knife to check if it's done. If the knife slides in easily all the way through, it's done. If not, put them back in the oven and let them cook for another 10 to 15 minutes, until they are all soft.

7. Leave the potatoes on the baking tray for 5 or 10 minutes after taking them out of the oven. When they are cool enough to touch (or you can put your oven gloves back on to move them), put them on a large plate or chopping board. Stick a fork into the side of the potato to hold it in place. With your other hand, use a knife to slice the potato lengthways down the middle, but only slice halfway through, until you've reached the fluffy insides, not all the way through to the bottom. After making the cut, use the fork to fluff up the insides.

8 Your crispy-skin baked potatoes are now ready for a slice of butter and a pinch of salt and pepper if you want to keep things simple. If you want to level up, try the two tasty jacket potato toppings on the next page.

TWO TASTY JACKET POTATO TOPPINGS

You can put just about anything on top of a baked potato (including our posh beans on page 65), but here are two of our favourite toppings to turn a simple jacket potato into a meal.

Makes 4

For the sour cream and chive topping:

100g sour cream

4 fresh chives

salt and pepper

For the chilli con carne topping:

250g leftover Bolognese (page 156)

1 x 400g tin of kidney beans

1 x 400g tin of chopped tomatoes (if needed to stretch your leftovers)

1 teaspoon ground cumin

½ teaspoon chilli powder

½ teaspoon smoked paprika

a pinch of cayenne pepper (optional)

30g Cheddar cheese

1. To make the sour cream and chive topping, put the sour cream in a small bowl. Use clean kitchen scissors to snip the chives into small pieces straight into the bowl. Add a little salt and pepper and stir it all together.

2. To serve, spoon the sour cream and chive mixture over the hot baked potatoes.

3. To make the chilli con carne topping, put your leftover Bolognese in a saucepan.

4. Put a colander in the sink. Empty the tin of beans into the colander, then rinse out the tin to catch any beans that are still hiding in there. Rinse the beans under cold running water until the water runs clear.

5. Add the rinsed beans to the pan along with the tin of tomatoes if needed – it depends on how much leftover Bolognese you have. Add the cumin, chilli powder, smoked paprika and cayenne (if using) and stir everything together.

6. Put the saucepan on the hob on a medium heat. Simmer for 10 to 15 minutes, until everything is heated up.

7. While that heats up, grate the cheese.

8. To serve, add spoonfuls of chilli con carne to each hot baked potato, then sprinkle a little grated Cheddar on top.

PERFECTLY COOKED PASTA

Did you know that different pasta shapes work best with certain sauces based on their texture, size and ability to hold onto the sauce?

Spaghetti and linguine are famously paired with Bolognese (page 156) and ragù, but are also best buddies with light, oil-based sauces like the aglio e olio on page 45 or creamy sauces like the carbonara on page 108.

Penne and rigatoni love thick sauces that fill their hollow centres, like the classic tomato sauce on page 46 or the arrabbiata sauce on page 48.

Fusilli has little twists and turns that make it work great with thick, creamy or chunky sauces that cling to every bite, like Lils's Bolognese on page 156.

Conchiglie, which is the Italian name for pasta shells, work with a pesto, like our homemade pesto rosso on page 82.

Macaroni are short, curved tubes that are essential in our mac 'n' cheese on page 107.

Farfalle is the bow tie-shaped pasta. Its name means 'butterfly' in Italian. Its sturdy texture and rigid centre make it great for salads, like our pasta salad on page 93.

When it comes to cooking spaghetti, we always use the twist trick. Dropping it into the saucepan with a gentle twist helps the strands fan out. It also prevents the pasta from sticking to the pan or clumping together as it cooks.

Our method for cooking pasta is unusual because we start it in cold water instead of adding it to boiling water. But trust us, it works! Plus we find this method works best for kids just starting out in the kitchen.

But there is one important rule that we do follow: never break the spaghetti! Italians take their pasta seriously, and breaking it is a big no-no. Spaghetti is meant to be twirled, not cut or snapped. I love slurping it up *Lady and the Tramp* style anyway.

RIGATONI

CONCHIGLIE

Our way of cooking pasta breaks all the rules, but it works! You can use any kind of pasta and any amount. The key is to add just enough cold water to cover it. A bonus is that there's very little water to drain at the end, just a small amount of starchy liquid that's perfect for adding to your sauce.

1. Put your pasta in a saucepan and add just enough cold water to cover the pasta. When cooking spaghetti, fill the saucepan halfway with water to start, as the spaghetti will stick out above the saucepan. Now add around 1 teaspoon of salt for every 100 grams of pasta – do some quick maths based on how much pasta your recipe is using.

2. Put the saucepan on the hob and turn the heat to high to boil the water. Using a wooden spoon or tongs, stir the pasta every minute or two while the water heats up so the pasta doesn't stick to the bottom of the pot or stick together.

3. As soon as the water starts to boil, set a timer for 10 minutes. Lower the heat so that the water is simmering, not boiling rapidly. Stir the pasta now and then while it cooks.

4. When the timer goes off, take one piece of pasta out of the pan using tongs or a slotted spoon and blow on it to cool it down. Test it: it should be soft but still slightly firm. The Italian way of saying this is al dente. If the pasta is still too hard, let it boil for another 3 to 5 minutes, until it's as soft as you like it.

5. Carefully dunk a mug or measuring jug into the cooking water to save some. A lot of recipes use this starchy cooking water in the pasta sauce.

6. Put a colander in the sink. Carefully drain the pasta by gently pouring the contents of the saucepan into it. Cooking the pasta this way makes it extra starchy, so rinse it with cold water, leaving you with the drained pasta in the colander.

7. Pop your drained pasta back into the saucepan to keep warm. If you need to keep it warm for more than a few minutes before using it, drizzle the pasta with a little olive oil so it doesn't stick together.

SPAGHETTI

MACARONI

FUSILLI

PENNE

FARFALLE

SPAGHETTI AGLIO E OLIO

Level up your perfectly cooked pasta into an easy aglio e olio, which means 'garlic and oil' in Italian. It usually uses spaghetti, but it works with any pasta shape.

Serves 2

200g spaghetti

2 garlic cloves

50g Parmesan cheese

a few sprigs of fresh parsley

3 tablespoons extra-virgin olive oil

¼ teaspoon chilli flakes (optional)

salt and pepper

1. Cook the spaghetti using the method on page 43, then drain it and put the spaghetti back in the saucepan.

2. While the pasta cooks, peel and grate the garlic, grate the Parmesan cheese and snip the parsley into tiny pieces.

3. Put the oil in a small frying pan, then put the pan on the hob on a low heat to let the oil warm up. Add the garlic and chilli flakes (if using) and cook for just 1 minute, until you can smell the garlic and it's starting to sizzle. Turn off the heat on the hob so the garlic doesn't burn, which would ruin the taste of the dish.

4. Pour your garlic and chilli oil over your drained pasta and mix using a wooden spoon or tongs. Add the grated Parmesan and snipped parsley, then add a little salt and pepper and mix again.

5. Divide the spaghetti aglio e olio between two plates and tuck in!

CLASSIC TOMATO SAUCE

A good tomato sauce is the base for so many dishes that we always have the ingredients for it in the kitchen. That's why when I'm hungry, it's one of my favourite things to rustle up.

We always add a little sugar to our tomato sauce because it helps to balance out the natural acidity in the tomatoes, which can sometimes make them taste bitter. But did you know that many jarred sauces are packed with sugar? By making your own, you control exactly how much goes in. And the best part? A classic tomato sauce not only tastes amazing, but it also counts as one of your five a day!

Serves 4

2 garlic cloves

2 tablespoons extra-virgin olive oil

2 x 400g tins of chopped tomatoes

a big handful of fresh basil leaves or 1 teaspoon dried basil

½ teaspoon dried oregano

1 tablespoon caster sugar

1 teaspoon salt

½ teaspoon black pepper

1. Peel and grate your garlic.

2. Put the olive oil in a saucepan, then put the pan on the hob on a low heat to let the oil warm up. Add the garlic and cook for just 1 minute, until you can smell it. Add the tomatoes, basil, oregano, sugar, salt and pepper and stir everything together.

3. With the pan still on a low heat, let the sauce simmer for 20 to 30 minutes, stirring now and then. You want the sauce to get a little thicker and all the flavours to get to know each other.

4. Your sauce is now ready to use, but you can put it in an airtight container in the fridge for up to five days. Or you can let it cool down, then put it in a freezerproof bag in the freezer for up to six months.

ARRABBIATA SAUCE

You can give a classic tomato sauce a twist in so many different ways by adding a few simple ingredients. One of the quickest and easiest ways is to turn it into an arrabbiata sauce.

Legend has it that when you eat this spicy sauce, your face turns red, like you're in the middle of a temper tantrum (but you never have one of those, right?). In Italian, arrabbiato means 'angry', but don't worry – this sauce is all about fiery flavour rather than rage. We're keeping the vibes chill, even if the heat isn't!

Serves 4

- 3 or 4 garlic cloves
- 2 tablespoons extra-virgin olive oil
- ¼ to ½ teaspoon chilli flakes
- 2 x 400g tins of chopped tomatoes
- a big handful of fresh basil leaves or 1 teaspoon dried basil
- ½ teaspoon dried oregano
- 1 tablespoon caster sugar
- 1 teaspoon salt
- ½ teaspoon black pepper
- 50ml cream (optional)

1 Peel and grate the garlic.

2 Put the oil in a medium-sized saucepan, then put the pan on a low heat on the hob and let the oil warm up. Add the grated garlic and ¼ teaspoon of chilli flakes and cook for 1 minute, just until you can smell the garlic and it's starting to sizzle. When adding chilli flakes, a little goes a long way, so start with a small amount. After you've tasted the sauce and if you're feeling brave, you can add a little more for an extra-fiery kick.

3 Stir in the tomatoes, basil, oregano, sugar, salt and pepper.

4 Simmer the sauce, still on a low heat, for 20 to 30 minutes, stirring now and then. You want the sauce to get a little thicker and all the flavours to get to know each other.

5 We like to add 50ml of cream sometimes, even though it's not traditional. Adding cream is also a helpful way to dial down the heat if you've accidentally made the sauce too spicy.

BR
FAST
BRU

EAK-
AND
NCH

CRUNCHY GRANOLA

Making your own crunchy granola is like stepping into history if you use a pestle and mortar – it's one of the oldest kitchen tools there is. The mortar is the heavy bowl and the pestle is the stick. (Even grown-ups still forget which one is which.) You use the pestle to smash and crush the nuts inside the mortar, just like cavemen and cavewomen did with their food. It's a fun way to mix things up, literally!

Makes 12 servings

100g mixed nuts (try almonds, cashews, hazelnuts, pecans, pistachios and/or walnuts)

300g jumbo oats

50g desiccated coconut

1 teaspoon ground cinnamon

½ teaspoon salt

180ml maple syrup or honey

3 tablespoons vegetable oil

1 teaspoon vanilla extract

100g mixed dried fruit (raisins, sultanas and/or dried cranberries)

1. Preheat your oven to 200°C for a conventional oven or 180°C for a fan oven.

2. Line a baking tray with non-stick baking paper.

3. To crush the nuts, put them in a pestle and mortar. Press and twist the pestle (the stick) to break them into smaller pieces, but not too small – you still want some chunky pieces. If you don't have a pestle and mortar, put the nuts in a ziplock bag, seal it closed and gently bash them with a rolling pin, which is still fun!

4. Put the crushed nuts, oats, coconut, cinnamon and salt in a large mixing bowl and stir together.

5. Put the maple syrup or honey, oil and vanilla in a separate small bowl or measuring jug and whisk together. Pour the wet ingredients over the dry ingredients and stir everything together.

6. Spread the mixture evenly onto the lined baking tray, then press it down firmly with a spatula.

7. Put the tray in the preheated oven and bake for 15 minutes. Using oven gloves, carefully remove the tray from the oven and put it on a wooden chopping board or on the hob to protect your countertop. Use a spatula to stir the granola, then spread it back out in an even layer and put it back in the oven to cook for 10 more minutes.

8. Use oven gloves again to remove the tray from the oven and put it on a wire rack. Let the granola cool completely, then add the mixed dried fruit. Use clean hands to break up any big clumps of granola and mix in the fruit.

9. Put your granola in an airtight container. It will stay fresh for up to two weeks.

TROPICAL BERRY SMOOTHIE BOWL

Our smoothie bowl recipe is just a guide, so get creative. Add your favourite fruits, nuts, seeds or even chocolate chips. Scatter, drizzle and dollop as much as you like. Just grab a bowl, and remember, the more colour, the more flavour. Like all good art, nothing is out of bounds (within reason, of course!).

Serves 2 to 4

300g frozen berries
100g frozen mango
200g natural Greek yogurt
1 tablespoon milk

Topping suggestions:

fresh raspberries and/or blueberries

sliced strawberries and/or sliced bananas

hazelnuts, pecans, flaked almonds and/or walnuts

a handful of granola (page 53)

a handful of raisins or chocolate chips

a handful of desiccated coconut

maple syrup or honey, to drizzle

1. Before you start, read the safety tips on how to use a blender on page 9.

2. Put your frozen fruit, yogurt and milk in a blender. Make sure the lid is on tight, then blend until smooth. Wait until the blender stops before taking the lid off and keep your hands away from the blades. Pour the smoothie into cereal bowls.

3. Now it's time to have fun! Add your favourite toppings, like fruit, nuts, granola, raisins, chocolate chips or coconut, then drizzle a little maple syrup or honey on top. And remember, the more colour, the better!

JAMMY EGGS AND TOAST SOLDIERS

The weekend has arrived, and with it, the perfect way to get it off to a cracking good start (see what I did there?): jammy eggs with crisp, buttery toast soldiers. Plus knowing how to cook perfectly soft-boiled eggs is a skill you'll use for life. I'm marching to the kitchen (in my PJs, of course) to make this.

Serves 2

2 large eggs

2 slices of bread (sliced white pan works perfectly)

30g salted butter

salt and pepper

1. Fill a saucepan with enough water to cover the eggs. Put the pan on the hob, turn the heat to high and bring to a boil.

2. Use a slotted spoon to carefully and slowly lower the eggs into the water to prevent cracking.

3. When the water starts boiling, set your timer for 6½ minutes exactly for perfectly soft-boiled eggs with jammy yolks.

4. While the eggs cook, fill a bowl with ice water.

5. As soon as the time is up, use the slotted spoon again to move the eggs to the bowl of ice water. Let them sit in the water for 2 minutes. This stops them from cooking any more while you prepare the soldiers.

6. Pop your bread into the toaster and toast until it's golden brown and crisp.

7. Spread the butter on the hot toast and let it melt into the bread, then use clean kitchen scissors to cut the toast into strips (soldiers) for dipping.

8. To serve, put each egg in an egg cup. Crack the top with a spoon and lift off the little shell 'lid'. Sprinkle with a little salt and pepper, then dip your buttery soldiers into that golden, jammy yolk.

ENORMOUS RASPBERRY SCONES

Ever wonder why scones grow so big in the oven? It's all thanks to a little kitchen chemistry. The yogurt here provides the acidity that reacts with the baking powder, which is alkaline. This reaction makes the lightest, fluffiest, most enormous scones. Who knew science could taste so good?

Makes 8 large (I mean enormous!) scones

450g self-raising flour, plus a little extra for the countertop

2 teaspoons baking powder

100g cold salted butter

80g caster sugar

500g natural Greek yogurt

1 teaspoon vanilla extract

100g fresh or frozen raspberries

1 egg

To serve:

butter

jam

squirty cream

1. Preheat your oven to 200°C for a conventional oven or 180°C for a fan oven.
2. Line two baking trays with non-stick baking paper.
3. To sift the flour into a large mixing bowl, put it in a large fine mesh sieve. Holding the handle of the sieve with one hand, and with the sieve raised up above the bowl, use your other hand to tap the side of the sieve so that the flour gently falls into the bowl. This gets air into the mix, which makes your scones extra fluffy.
4. Sift the baking powder into the bowl the same way. The baking powder adds extra 'enormousness', but so does the air that you just added to the mixture by sifting.
5. Using the large holes on a box grater, grate the cold butter straight into the flour. Using your fingertips, rub the butter into the flour until it looks like breadcrumbs.
6. Add the sugar and give it all a stir with a wooden spoon. Add the yogurt and vanilla extract and stir again to bring everything together.
7. Finally, add the raspberries. Use a spatula to carefully lift and turn the dough over itself to gently mix in the raspberries. You don't want them to break up too much or they will make the dough too wet.
8. Sprinkle your countertop with a little flour. Tip the dough onto the floured work surface and sprinkle your hands with flour too, then shape the dough into a ball. If the dough is too sticky, sprinkle a little more flour on it.
9. Flatten the dough with your hands or a rolling pin until it's 2cm to 3cm thick.
10. Cut out eight scones using a 6cm cutter or the rim of a large drinking glass. Put them on the lined baking trays, leaving 3cm to 4cm of space between them to give them room to grow in the oven.

11 Crack the egg into a small bowl, then whisk with a fork. Using a pastry brush, paint the tops of the scones with the beaten egg to give them a golden shine.

12 Put the trays in the preheated oven and bake for 20 to 25 minutes, checking the scones after 20 minutes. They should be light golden and they should have grown enormous. To check if they're done, tap the bottom of a scone – if it sounds hollow, they're ready.

13 Using oven gloves, carefully remove the trays from the oven and put them on a wooden chopping board or on the hob to protect your countertop. Let the scones cool for a few minutes, then put them on wire racks to cool a little more.

14 Enjoy your enormous scones with butter, jam and maybe a little squirty cream.

FLIPPING GREAT BUTTERMILK PANCAKES

The secret to making perfect pancakes starts with a good non-stick pan. It will literally make or break your pancakes. Here's another important tip: when sifting your dry ingredients, hold your sieve nice and high above the bowl. This gets air into the mix, making your pancakes extra fluffy. Oh, and one final tip: expect the first pancake to turn out a bit wonky. It happens to everyone!

Makes 4

200g self-raising flour

1 teaspoon baking powder

50g caster sugar

250ml buttermilk

2 eggs

1 teaspoon vanilla extract

a little oil or butter, for cooking

To serve:

fresh berries

maple syrup

squirty cream

1. To sift the flour and baking powder into a large mixing bowl, put them in a large fine mesh sieve. Holding the handle of the sieve with one hand, and with the sieve raised up nice and high above the bowl, use your other hand to tap the side of the sieve so that the flour gently falls into the bowl.

2. Add the sugar to the bowl and stir everything together.

3. Measure the buttermilk in a large measuring jug, then crack the eggs into the jug, add the vanilla and whisk the wet ingredients together.

4. Make a well in the middle of your dry ingredients, then pour in the buttermilk mixture. Whisk until you have a smooth batter.

5. Pour a little oil into a non-stick frying pan (or spray oil is great for pancakes) or add a little butter. Put the pan on a medium heat. Let the oil warm up for a few minutes or let the butter melt, then pour in a small ladleful of the batter. Turn the heat down to low to make sure your pancakes don't burn.

6. So how do you know when to flip the pancake? When bubbles and holes start to appear on top of the pancake and the edges turn slightly brown, that's your signal. Gently slide your spatula under the pancake, making sure the pancake is fully supported before lifting it. You can do this!

7. Lift the pancake about 5cm above the pan, then turn your wrist quickly but gently to flip the pancake over. Don't worry if your first few flips aren't perfect. Practice makes perfect!

8. Cook the other side for 2 minutes, then use your spatula again to lift the pancake out of the pan and onto a plate. Cook the rest of the pancakes the same way.

9. Stack your pancakes up and serve with your favourite toppings. Strawberries, blueberries, raspberries, maple syrup and squirty cream are ours.

BREAKFAST AND BRUNCH

CINNAMON FRENCH TOAST HUGS

If I had to describe the flavour of a hug, it would be cinnamon. It's warm and comforting, just like a hug from my mum (but don't tell her I said that). Making cinnamon French toast for your friends, family or yourself is like giving a giant, cosy hug. It's perfect for making for Mother's Day, Father's Day or when you've had a tough week at school and need a little pick-me-up. But if you're not into cinnamon (or hugs!), there's always chocolate spread.

Makes 4 slices

50ml milk

2 eggs

1 teaspoon ground cinnamon

1 teaspoon vanilla extract

4 slices of brioche or sliced white bread

1 tablespoon vegetable oil

25g salted butter

For the cinnamon sugar:

½ teaspoon caster sugar

½ teaspoon ground cinnamon

To serve:

your favourite fresh fruit

1 To make the cinnamon sugar, put the sugar and cinnamon in a small bowl and stir them together.

2 To make the French toast, measure the milk in a large measuring jug. Crack the eggs into the jug, then add the cinnamon and vanilla. Whisk until smooth.

3 Put the bread slices side by side in a large, shallow baking dish. Pour the egg mixture over the bread and let it soak for 3 minutes, then flip the bread over and soak the other side for 2 minutes.

4 Meanwhile, put the oil and butter in a non-stick frying pan. Put the pan on a medium heat on the hob. When the butter has melted and started to bubble a little, the pan is hot enough.

5 Using a spatula, lift one slice of bread at a time out of the baking dish and into the pan. Cook each slice for 2 minutes on each side, until crisp and golden. (You can count to 120 in your head while you wait.)

6 To serve, put the French toast on a plate and sprinkle some cinnamon sugar on top. Add a handful of your favourite fresh fruit.

POSH BEANS ON TOAST

'Beans, beans are good for the heart, the more you eat, the more you...' well, you know the rest. But these are posh beans on toast, so try not to burst into the classic beans song while whipping up this fancy-schmancy dish. No promises, though ... wink wink!

Serves 2

20g mature Cheddar cheese

1 x 400g tin of butter beans

200g tomato passata

1 teaspoon smoked paprika

1 teaspoon Worcestershire sauce

salt and pepper

2 tablespoons crème fraîche or sour cream

2 slices of sourdough bread

30g salted butter

1. Grate the cheese on a box grater. Put the cheese in a small bowl and set it aside.

2. Open the tin of butter beans, dump them into a sieve and rinse them under cold running water. Shake them off, Taylor Swift style.

3. Put the butter beans in a small saucepan, then put the pan on a medium heat on the hob. Add the passata, paprika, Worcestershire and a little salt and pepper and let the beans simmer for 1 minute.

4. Put the crème fraîche or sour cream in a small bowl. Take a spoonful of the warm bean mixture and stir it into the crème fraîche or sour cream to gently warm it up. This prevents it from curdling when you add it to the beans. Add the mixture to the beans, turn the heat down to low and let it simmer for 5 minutes.

5. Meanwhile, toast your sourdough. While it's still hot, spread half of the butter on each slice.

6. To serve, put a piece of buttered toast on each plate, then spoon half of the beans on top of each slice. Finish by sprinkling the grated Cheddar on top. And all together now: 'Beans, beans, they're good for the heart...'

SAUSAGE AND EGG MUFFINS

The best thing about these sausage and egg muffins is that you can make them anytime, whether it's for breakfast, lunch or as an after-school snack. Or if you want to make them for a play date and impress your friends, wrap them up in non-stick baking paper, and you've got the perfect package that looks like it came from a drive-thru.

Makes 4

450g sausage meat

1 tablespoon plain flour, plus a little extra for your hands

1 tablespoon dried sage

1 tablespoon olive oil

25g salted butter

4 eggs

4 slices of cheese

4 pre-sliced English muffins

To serve:

a little ketchup (optional)

1. Preheat your oven to 200°C for a conventional oven or 180°C for a fan oven.

2. Line two baking trays with non-stick baking paper.

3. Put the sausage meat in a large mixing bowl with the flour to make it less sticky. Add the sage, then use clean hands to gently mix everything together.

4. Wash your hands with warm soapy water and pat them dry with a tea towel. Sprinkle a little flour on your hands, then shape the sausage meat into four burger patties about 2cm thick. If the mixture is still too sticky, add a little more flour. Put the sausage patties on one of the lined baking trays.

5. Put the tray in the preheated oven and cook for 15 minutes, until the sausage patties are golden and crispy.

6. Meanwhile, pour the oil into a medium-sized non-stick frying pan and use a pastry brush or a piece of kitchen paper to spread it around. This helps prevent any hot oil from splattering. Add the butter and put the pan on a medium heat on the hob. When the butter has melted and started to bubble, the pan is hot enough.

7. Crack each egg onto a saucer to avoid any splashes when you add it to the pan. Carefully slide the eggs into the hot pan and fry for 4 minutes if you want a runny yolk or 6 minutes for a set yolk.

8. Using oven gloves, carefully remove the tray from the oven and put it on a wooden chopping board or on the hob to protect your countertop. Put a slice of cheese on top of each sausage patty, then put the tray back in the oven and cook for 5 more minutes, until the cheese melts.

9. Put the English muffins on the second baking tray, cut sides facing up, then pop the tray into the oven to toast them while the sausage patties finish cooking.

10 Assemble the muffins by spreading a little ketchup on the bottom half of each toasted English muffin if you like, then top it with a sausage patty and a fried egg. Sandwich together with the toasted top halves and serve immediately.

EGG MAYONNAISE ON TOASTED BAGELS

Not to brag, but I'm a master egg peeler. Mum says it's my special talent, and honestly, I sometimes imagine going on a TV talent show with it:

Judge: Name?

Me: Lily Mae Cox.

Judge: Age?

Me: Eleven.

Judge: What's your talent?

Me: Peeling hard-boiled eggs.

Judge (gasps impressively): Off you go!

We've got an egg-peeling tip to help you out, but with your nimble little fingers, you're already at an advantage compared to grown-ups.

Makes 2

4 eggs

salt and pepper

4 spring onions or fresh chives

3 tablespoons mayonnaise

2 bagels

a little butter for each bagel

1. Gently put the eggs in a medium-sized saucepan and cover them with cold water. Put the saucepan on a high heat on the hob and bring the water to a boil.

2. When the water is boiling, reduce the heat to medium and set a timer for 10 minutes exactly. This will give you perfectly hard-boiled eggs.

3. While the eggs cook, fill a bowl with ice water and have it ready to go.

4. When the 10 minutes are up, remove the eggs from the saucepan with a slotted spoon. You'll know they're ready when the water evaporates instantly from the shells. Put the eggs in the bowl of ice water to cool them down, which makes them easier to peel.

5. To peel the eggs, tap the large end of each egg to crack it. There's a small air pocket there that gives you a good grip for peeling the shell off.

6. Put all the peeled eggs in a clean medium-sized bowl. Break them up with a fork, leaving some larger chunks for texture. Add a little salt and pepper.

7   Use clean kitchen scissors to snip the green tops of the spring onions or chives into small pieces right into the bowl. Stir in the mayonnaise, then taste to see if it needs any more salt or pepper.

8   To prepare your bagels, lay them flat on your chopping board and put your hand on top to steady the bagel. Use a serrated bread knife in a gentle sawing motion to cut it horizontally through the centre. (Some bagels come pre-sliced, so keep an eye out for those.)

9   Lightly toast your bagels – don't let them get too brown.

10 To serve, spread a little butter on each bagel half, then divide the egg mayo between the two bottom halves. Sandwich together with the toasted top halves.

EPIC HAM AND CHEESE TOASTIE

The secrets to an epic toastie are simple. First, start with plain white bread, not that fancy seeded stuff grown-ups always seem to buy. Then take this toastie to the next level by using two types of cheese: Cheddar for the flavour and fresh mozzarella for that perfect melty cheese pull. Add two good slices of ham, and you've just unlocked top-level toastie status.

Makes 1

50g fresh mozzarella cheese (from a ball)

50g mature Cheddar cheese

2 slices of white bread

50g salted butter, plus a little extra for cooking

2 slices of ham

To serve:

a handful of crisps

1. Drain off the water from the ball of fresh mozzarella. Use your hands to tear 50g of the cheese into strips and put them in a bowl.

2. Grate the Cheddar. Put it in the bowl with the mozzarella and mix the two cheeses together.

3. Put both slices of bread side by side on a chopping board.

4. If your butter is straight from the fridge, use the box grater to grate it into a bowl. This makes it easier to spread. Spread half of the butter on one slice of bread, then put the bread on the board, butter side down. Repeat with the second slice of bread.

5. Scatter the cheeses over the non-buttered side of one piece of bread. Put the ham on top of the cheese. Put the second slice of bread on top, buttered side up, to complete your sandwich.

6. Put a non-stick frying pan on a medium heat on the hob. Add a little butter (this is called a knob of butter). When the butter has melted and started to bubble a little, the pan is hot enough.

7. Slide a spatula under the sandwich, then carefully lift your sandwich into the pan. Using the spatula, gently press it down and enjoy the sound of that buttery sizzle.

8. Cook for 2 to 3 minutes. Use the spatula to lift the sandwich up after 2 minutes to see if the bottom slice of bread is golden brown. When it is, use the spatula to flip the sandwich over and fry the other side. Give it another gentle press to help the cheese melt beautifully. Cook for 2 to 3 minutes more, until that side is golden too.

9. When both sides are golden and the cheese is melted and gooey, use your spatula to remove the toastie from the pan and put it on a plate.

10 Cut the toastie in half with clean kitchen scissors. You could add a handful of crisps on the side like they do in cafés. Now devour that gooey, cheesy deliciousness, preferably alone in your room, where no one can steal a bite.

LU

LOVE YOUR LUNCHBOX

APPLE AND BANANA OAT BAKES

We've been making these apple and banana oat bakes ever since I started pre-school, and guess what? I still love them. These will keep you fuelled from little break all the way to big lunch. They're packed with fruit and oats, so they're secretly healthy, but you can always throw in a few chocolate chips as a treat.

Makes 12

100g salted butter

2 ripe bananas

2 apples

200g porridge oats

100g raisins or sultanas

3 tablespoons maple syrup or honey

1 teaspoon vanilla extract

1 egg

1. Preheat your oven to 200°C for a conventional oven or 180°C for a fan oven.

2. Line a 23cm x 33cm baking tin with non-stick baking paper (read page 6 for tips on how to line a rectangular tin).

3. Put the butter in a small saucepan. Put the pan on a medium-low heat on the hob and let the butter melt. Or you can put the butter in a heatproof bowl and microwave it for 1 minute to melt it.

4. Peel the bananas and put them in a large mixing bowl. Use a fork or potato masher to squish them really well.

5. Peel and grate the apples, then add them to the mashed bananas. Add the oats and the raisins or sultanas and give everything a good mix.

6. Pour in the melted butter, maple syrup or honey and the vanilla, then crack in the egg. Use a wooden spoon to stir everything together.

7. Scrape the mixture into the lined baking tin. Run your hands under the tap, then use your damp hands to pat the mixture into an even layer all the way to the edges of the tin.

8. Put the tin in the preheated oven and bake for about 20 minutes, until golden brown on top. If you think it isn't golden enough, let it bake for 5 more minutes.

9. Using oven gloves, carefully remove the tin from the oven and put it on a wire cooling rack. Allow to cool completely to make them easier to slice, then use the paper to lift the slab out of the tin and onto a chopping board. Cut into 12 bars.

10. Store the bars in an airtight container for up to four days – if they last that long.

FIVE-A-DAY LUNCHBOX MUFFINS

These sneaky little muffins are jam-packed with fruit and veg – but you wouldn't even know it if you weren't making these yourself. They're like undercover veggies, slipping into your lunchbox disguised as a treat. Watch out, though – not only will these muffins make your lunchbox legendary, they might also cause your parents to break out in an embarrassing happy dance when another empty lunchbox comes home.

Makes 12

1 ripe banana

1 apple

1 carrot

½ courgette

50g sultanas or raisins

2 eggs

80g dark brown sugar

4 tablespoons vegetable or olive oil, plus extra for greasing the muffin tin if you're not using paper liners

1 teaspoon vanilla extract

200g self-raising flour

1 teaspoon baking powder

½ teaspoon ground ginger

½ teaspoon ground cinnamon

1. Preheat your oven to 200°C for a conventional oven or 180°C for a fan oven.

2. Line a 12-hole muffin tin with paper liners (read page 6 for how to make your own bakery-style liners) or lightly grease each hole by putting a little oil on a piece of kitchen paper, then use the paper to rub the bottom and sides of each hole. Or if you have a silicone muffin tray, use that, but still grease the holes.

3. Peel the banana and put it in a large mixing bowl. Use a fork or potato masher to squish it really well.

4. Peel and grate the apple and carrot. Grate the courgette (you don't have to peel it), then add them all to the mashed banana. Add the sultanas or raisins, then stir together with a wooden spoon.

5. Crack the eggs into the bowl, then add the dark brown sugar, oil and vanilla and stir everything together.

6. To sift the dry ingredients, put the flour, baking powder, ginger and cinnamon in a large fine mesh sieve. Holding the handle of the sieve with one hand, and with the sieve raised up above the bowl, use your other hand to tap the side of the sieve so that the flour gently falls into the bowl. This gets air into the mix, making your muffins extra fluffy. Use your wooden spoon again to mix everything together.

7. Use a spoon or an ice cream scoop to divide the batter evenly among the 12 holes in the muffin tin, filling each one only three-quarters full.

8. Put the muffin tin on a baking tray to make it easier to get it in and out of the oven, especially if you've used a silicone tray. Put the tin in the preheated oven and bake for 20 to 25 minutes, until a toothpick inserted into the centre of a muffin comes out clean.

9. Using oven gloves, carefully remove the tin from the oven and put it on a wire cooling rack. Let the muffins cool in the tin for 10 minutes before taking them out of the tin and putting them on the rack to cool completely. If you haven't used paper liners, you might need to run a butter knife around the edges of the muffins to loosen them from the tin.

10. Let the muffins cool completely before putting them in an airtight container. They will keep for up to four days at room temperature.

MINI CHEESE SCONES

These are the easiest, cheesiest scones you'll ever make. After your first batch, you'll wonder why people ever buy scones in the shops. Just a heads up: your mum or dad will definitely try to sneak some for their tea, so you might want to hide a few to make sure you have some left for your lunchbox.

Makes 20

50g Cheddar cheese

200g self-raising flour, plus extra for the countertop

1 teaspoon baking powder

100g cold salted butter

200g natural Greek yogurt

1 egg

1. Preheat your oven to 200°C for a conventional oven or 180°C for a fan oven.

2. Line two baking trays with non-stick baking paper, because nobody likes scraping scones off a tray (yes, that is experience talking).

3. Grate the Cheddar.

4. To sift the flour and baking powder into a large mixing bowl, put them in a large fine mesh sieve. Holding the handle of the sieve with one hand, and with the sieve raised up above the bowl, use your other hand to tap the side of the sieve so that the flour and baking powder gently fall into the bowl. This gets air into the mix, making your scones extra fluffy.

5. Using the large holes on a box grater, grate the cold butter straight into the flour. Using your fingertips, rub the butter into the flour until it looks like breadcrumbs.

6. Add the yogurt and grated Cheddar, then stir everything together with a wooden spoon until you have a ball of dough.

7. Scatter a small handful of flour over your clean countertop so the dough doesn't stick to it. Tip the dough out of the bowl onto the countertop. Put a little flour on your hands and use them to pat down the dough until it's about 2cm thick.

8. Use a 4cm scone cutter or the rim of an egg cup to stamp out the mini scones. There will still be dough left over, so form it into a ball, flatten it down again and stamp out a few more. Repeat until you've used up all the dough. Put the scones on the lined baking trays, spaced a few centimetres apart to give them room to puff up in the oven.

9. Crack the egg into a small bowl, then whisk it with a fork. Use a pastry brush to paint the top of each scone with the egg wash. This will make them turn golden and shiny.

10. Put the trays in the preheated oven and bake for 20 minutes, until the scones are golden and smell amazing.

11 Using oven gloves, carefully remove the trays from the oven and put them on a wire rack. Let the scones cool completely before storing in an airtight container for up to four days at room temperature. But good luck waiting for them to cool – these are impossible to resist when they're still warm from the oven.

SMOKED SALMON AND CREAM CHEESE PINWHEELS

This can be made in minutes the night before, then left to happily chill out in the fridge overnight, waiting to be sliced and packed in your lunchbox. If you're not a fan of smoked salmon, ham slices work too. Get ready to wrap and roll (I swear that was my mum's joke, not mine).

Serves 1

1 large flour tortilla wrap

a big spoonful of cream cheese

2 slices of smoked salmon or cooked ham

2 spring onions or 4 fresh chives

1 small gherkin or cornichon

salt and pepper

1. Put your wrap on a chopping board. Put a big spoonful of cream cheese in the middle, then spread it all over the wrap, going almost all the way to the edges.

2. Put the smoked salmon or ham on the edge of the tortilla that's closest to you.

3. Use clean kitchen scissors to snip the green tops of the spring onions or the chives into small pieces, then snip the gherkin or cornichon into small pieces too. Sprinkle the chopped spring onions or chives and the chopped gherkin on top of the smoked salmon or ham, then add a little salt and pepper.

4. Roll up the tortilla tightly, like a Swiss roll. Wrap the roll in foil and leave it in the fridge overnight. This will help the pinwheels keep their shape.

5. In the morning, take the wrap out of the foil and use scissors to cut the wrap into four pinwheels. Line your pinwheels back up, wrap them back up in the foil and put them in your lunchbox.

PESTO ROSSO

Pesto rosso (also called sun-dried tomato pesto or red pesto) is the secret weapon of the lunchbox. We don't just use it as a sauce for pasta in a hot food flask, though it's pretty great that way. Pesto rosso is a lunchtime hero because it tastes amazing even when it's cold. You can use it as a dip for breadsticks or as a spread to make rolls or sandwiches extra tasty – it can even rescue a boring ham and cheese sandwich. Plus it's the ultimate dip for the mini quiches on page 90 and the jambons on page 86. Whatever you put it with, pesto rosso will take your lunch from meh to amazing.

Makes 800ml

50g Parmesan cheese

4 large roasted red peppers from a jar

200g sun-dried tomatoes from a jar

60g pine nuts

the leaves from a few sprigs of fresh basil

2 tablespoons tomato purée

1 teaspoon dried oregano

salt and pepper

1 tablespoon olive oil, if needed

1. Before you start, read the safety tips on how to use a blender on page 9.

2. Grate the Parmesan cheese.

3. Now just pop the cheese, peppers, tomatoes, pine nuts, basil, tomato purée, oregano and a big pinch of salt and pepper into the blender. Add the oil from the jar of sun-dried tomatoes to the blender too. Make sure the blender lid is clicked on properly, then blitz until you've got a smooth paste. Add a tablespoon of olive oil if the pesto is too thick and needs some help to all blend together.

4. Store the pesto in a clean, sealed jar in the fridge for up to a week, perfect for dips, as a pasta sauce or for jazzing up sandwiches and rolls.

TURKEY NUGGET CIABATTAS

These mini turkey nuggets are so tasty on their own that they're perfect for a lunchbox pick-and-mix alongside veggie buddies like carrot sticks, cucumber batons and pepper strips, with a little pot of ketchup on the side for dipping. But add them to a ciabatta with homemade pesto rosso and grated mozzarella, and bam, you've got the ultimate sandwich.

Makes 4

50g Cheddar cheese
50g Parmesan cheese
200g fresh breadcrumbs
1 tablespoon dried oregano
1 teaspoon garlic powder
salt and pepper
400g turkey mince

To serve:

4 ciabattas
pesto rosso (page 82)
100g grated mozzarella

1. Preheat your oven to 200°C for a conventional oven or 180°C for a fan oven.

2. Line a baking tray with non-stick baking paper.

3. Grate the Cheddar and Parmesan. Put the two cheeses in a large mixing bowl with the breadcrumbs, oregano, garlic powder and a little salt and pepper and stir together.

4. Add the turkey mince, then roll up your sleeves and use your clean hands to mix everything together.

5. Divide the mixture into 24 x 30g portions. Roll each one into a ball, then flatten it into an oval-shaped nugget and put them on the lined baking tray.

6. Put the tray in the preheated oven and cook for 20 minutes, until the nuggets are golden and cooked through.

7. Using oven gloves, carefully remove the tray from the oven and put it on a wire cooling rack. Let the nuggets cool completely before putting them in a sandwich if you're making these ahead of time.

8. To cut each ciabatta in half, put them flat on a chopping board. Working with one at a time, put your hand on top and slice it horizontally through the centre using a gentle sawing motion with a serrated bread knife.

9. Spread a little pesto on the top and bottom of each ciabatta. Sprinkle a little grated mozzarella over each bottom half. Add some cooked turkey nuggets and sandwich together with the top half. Wrap each roll in greaseproof paper for an extra-special touch. Any leftover nuggets can be frozen in a freezerproof bag or saved for an after-school snack.

JAMBONS

A jambon is a flaky pastry stuffed with ham and melty cheese – the ultimate lunchtime snack. It may have a French-sounding name (the word 'jambon' just means 'ham', by the way), but jambons are one of the most popular grab-and-go snacks in Ireland. Here's our simple homemade version that has a special place in our Irish hearts and tummies too.

Makes 12

2 sheets of ready-rolled puff pastry

150g mature white Cheddar cheese

100g cooked ham

1 x 250g tub of mascarpone cheese

1 teaspoon Dijon mustard

½ teaspoon ground nutmeg

1 egg

1. If your pastry is frozen, put it in the fridge overnight to thaw it.

2. The next day, preheat your oven to 200°C for a conventional oven or 180°C for a fan oven.

3. Line two baking trays with non-stick baking paper.

4. Grate the Cheddar. Cut the ham into small pieces using clean kitchen scissors.

5. Unroll the puff pastry sheets on a chopping board. Cut each sheet in half lengthways, then into thirds widthways so that you get six small rectangles on each sheet.

6. Put the mascarpone cheese, mustard and nutmeg in a large mixing bowl and stir with a wooden spoon. Add the grated Cheddar and diced ham and stir together.

7. Put a generous tablespoon of the ham and cheese mixture in the middle of each puff pastry rectangle. Fold in the corners to create little parcels. Put the parcels on the lined baking trays, spaced apart to give them room to puff up a little.

8. Crack the egg into a small bowl, then whisk with a fork. Using a pastry brush, paint the top of each parcel with the beaten egg to give them a golden shine.

9. Put the trays in the preheated oven and bake for 30 minutes, until the jambons are puffed up and golden. Don't worry if some of the filling oozes out the sides.

10. Using oven gloves, carefully remove the trays from the oven and put them on a wire cooling rack. Let the jambons cool completely before putting them in an airtight container. They will keep in the fridge for up to three days, ready to pack into your lunchbox.

PORK AND APPLE SAUSAGE ROLLS

All your pals will be drooling when you lift your lunchbox lid to reveal these sausage rolls. Trust me, they'll be lining up for a lunchbox trade-off. So who's ready to roll?

Makes 8

1 sheet of ready-rolled puff pastry

2 spring onions or fresh chives

16 pork sausages or 450g sausage meat

1 apple

1 garlic clove

1 heaped teaspoon dried sage

salt and pepper

1 egg

1 tablespoon sesame seeds (optional)

1. If your pastry is frozen, put it in the fridge overnight to thaw it.

2. The next day, preheat your oven to 200°C for a conventional oven or 180°C for a fan oven.

3. Line a baking tray with non-stick baking paper.

4. Use clean kitchen scissors to snip the green tops of the spring onions or the chives into small pieces straight into a large mixing bowl.

5. Using the kitchen scissors again, cut the sausages apart at the string in between each one, then line them up. Find the loose end of the sausage casing and make a small cut to start peeling it off. Gently remove the casing from all the sausages and put the meat in the mixing bowl. Or you can skip this step if you're using sausage meat.

6. Peel and grate the apple and garlic. Put them in the mixing bowl, then add the sage and a little salt and pepper. Mix everything together with your clean hands.

7. Wash your hands with warm soapy water, then unroll the sheet of puff pastry onto a chopping board. Cut it in half lengthways, then cut it into quarters widthways so that you get eight rectangles.

8. Divide the sausage mixture into eight portions, then roll each one into a sausage shape. Put one portion along the long edge of one puff pastry rectangle. Roll the pastry over the sausage, pressing the edges down with a fork to seal them together. Put the roll on the lined baking tray. Repeat with the rest of the sausage and pastry, making sure the rolls are spaced at least 2cm apart from each other on the tray.

9. Crack the egg into a small bowl, then whisk with a fork. Use a pastry brush to paint the top of each sausage roll with the beaten egg to make them nice and golden. Sprinkle the sesame seeds on top (if using).

10. Put the tray in the preheated oven and bake for 30 minutes, until the pastry is golden and the sausage is fully cooked.

11. Using oven gloves, carefully remove the tray from the oven and put it on a wire cooling rack. Let the sausage rolls cool completely before putting them in an airtight container. They will keep in the fridge for up to three days, ready to pack into your lunchbox.

MINI QUICHES

These mini quiches are so tasty, I always try to pack an extra one for my bestie. Here's a cool tip: get a 12-hole silicone muffin tray. You can find these in any kitchen shop or bargain store, and they make it super easy to pop the mini quiches out when they're done. (It will also work for the five-a-day lunchbox muffins on page 76.)

Makes 12

1 sheet of ready-rolled shortcrust pastry

1 tablespoon olive oil

3 eggs

salt and pepper

2 slices of ham

100g grated Cheddar and mozzarella mix

1. If your pastry is frozen, put it in the fridge overnight to thaw it.

2. The next day, preheat your oven to 200°C for a conventional oven or 180°C for a fan oven.

3. Grease the holes in a muffin tin or silicone muffin tray by putting the tablespoon of oil on a piece of kitchen paper, then using the paper to rub the bottom and sides of each hole.

4. Unroll the pastry onto a chopping board. Cut it into rounds about 7cm wide by putting a mug upside-down on the pastry and tracing the tip of a knife around the edge. Put one pastry round in each hole of the muffin tin. It should cover the bottom and come about halfway up the sides of each hole. If it doesn't, use a rolling pin to roll out each disc to make it a little bigger.

5. Crack the eggs into a measuring jug. Add a little salt and pepper, then whisk with a fork.

6. Cut the ham into small pieces using clean kitchen scissors.

7. Carefully pour some of the beaten egg into each pastry round until it's about three-quarters full – don't overfill!

8. Sprinkle some diced ham and grated cheese on top.

9. Put the muffin tin on a baking tray to make it easier to get it in and out of the oven, especially if you've used a silicone tray. Put in the preheated oven and cook for 25 to 30 minutes, until the mini quiches are golden and puffed up.

10. Using oven gloves, carefully remove the tin from the oven and put it on a wire cooling rack. Let the quiches cool for 5 or 10 minutes before carefully popping them out of the tin. If you haven't used a silicone tray, you might need to run a butter knife around the edges of the quiches to loosen them from the tin.

11 Put the mini quiches on the wire cooling rack and let them get completely cold before putting them in an airtight container. They will keep in the fridge for up to three days, ready to pack into your lunchbox.

CREAMY, CRUNCHY PASTA SALAD

This isn't just any pasta salad, it's THE pasta salad, the only one I eat. It's creamy, crunchy, sweet and savoury – basically, it's everything you never knew you needed in one bowl. The combo of honey and mayo is what makes it pure magic. Now, I know what you're thinking. Honey and mayo?! It's weird but wonderful, like pineapple on pizza. Don't knock it till you try it! Seriously, this is so good, you'll forget that it's technically a salad.

Serves 4

500g farfalle (also called bow tie pasta, but any shape will work)
6 tablespoons honey
6 tablespoons mayonnaise
2 red peppers
1 small cucumber
1 x 160g tin of sweetcorn
salt and pepper

1. Cook the pasta using the method on page 43.
2. While the pasta is cooking, put the honey and mayo in a large mixing bowl and whisk them together.
3. Dice the red peppers. Make cucumber ribbons with a peeler, then cut those ribbons into smaller strips using clean kitchen scissors.
4. Put a colander in the sink, then drain the sweetcorn. Put it in the bowl with the mayo and honey.
5. When the timer goes for the pasta, drain it in the colander in the sink. Run it under cold water to cool it down. Shake off any water that might still be sticking to the pasta, then put it in the bowl with the honey and mayo.
6. Toss in the red pepper and cucumber. Add a little salt and pepper, then stir until everything is coated in that honey mayo magic.
7. Divide the pasta salad among four airtight containers. It will keep for up to three days stored in the fridge, ready for packing into your lunchbox.

AF
SCH

TER–
OOL
UEL

CHOPPED CHICKEN WRAP

My favourite wrap filling is the classic combo of chicken, iceberg lettuce and cucumber, but once you've mastered the technique of rolling up a wrap, the possibilities are endless. And if you chop all your fillings nice and small, every bite gives you a perfect taste of everything.

Two other filling combos to try are smoked salmon + avocado + cream cheese + Baby Gem lettuce or ham + grated Cheddar + tomato (remove the seeds) + mayo + butterhead lettuce.

Makes 1

1 large flour tortilla wrap

1 tablespoon mayonnaise

1 tablespoon sweet chilli sauce

40g cucumber

50g cooked chicken slices

40g iceberg lettuce

a handful of grated Cheddar and mozzarella mix

1. Spread the tortilla wrap with the mayonnaise and sweet chilli sauce.

2. Cut the cucumber into thin slices.

3. Put the cooked chicken and the lettuce on the chopping board with the cucumber slices. Finely chop everything together using the scatter or mezzaluna method on page 23.

4. Mum says I'm a master at wrapping wraps, so here are my top tips. Put all the chopped filling ingredients in the middle of the wrap, slightly off-centre towards one side. Keep the filling about 5cm from the edges to avoid overstuffing, which can make a messy wrap.

5. Sprinkle the grated cheese over the filling.

6. Fold in the left and right edges to cover the ends of the filling, keeping everything neatly tucked in.

7. Next, fold the bottom edge snugly over the filling to hold it all together.

8. Then, while keeping the sides tucked in, roll the wrap tightly from the bottom to the top, making sure it's firm but not so tight that the tortilla tears.

9. If you're having this after school, cut it in half and tuck in. But if you want to bring it for your packed lunch, wrap the whole thing tightly in a piece of foil, then cut it in half and put it in an airtight container, ready for your lunchbox.

TUNA AND SWEETCORN MELT

I'll be honest: tuna wouldn't be my first choice for a sandwich. But my mum insists that lots of kids love tuna, so she says you might enjoy this as an after-school snack. That said, you can use tinned salmon or cooked chicken if, like me, you're not a fan of tuna.

Makes 2

1 x 80g tin of tuna

60g tinned sweetcorn

2 small gherkins

1 tablespoon brine from the jar of gherkins

1 tablespoon mayonnaise

1 tablespoon ketchup

2 small ciabattas

25g grated Cheddar and mozzarella mix

1. Preheat your oven to 200°C for a conventional oven or 180°C for a fan oven.

2. Line a baking tray with non-stick baking paper.

3. Put a colander in the sink. Carefully open the tins of tuna and sweetcorn, then drain them both. Put the tuna and sweetcorn in a large mixing bowl.

4. Using clean kitchen scissors, snip the gherkins into the bowl.

5. Add the gherkin brine (in other words, the juice from the pickle jar), mayonnaise and ketchup and stir everything together.

6. To cut the ciabattas in half, lay them flat on your chopping board. Working with one at a time, put your hand on top to steady it. Use a serrated bread knife in a gentle sawing motion to cut it horizontally through the centre. (Some ciabattas come pre-sliced, so keep an eye out for those.) Put the two halves on the lined tray, cut sides facing up.

7. Divide the tuna mixture between the two bottom halves, then sprinkle half of the grated cheese on top of each one.

8. Put the tray in the preheated oven and cook 10 minutes, until the cheese is melted and golden.

9. Using oven gloves, carefully remove the tray from the oven and put it on a wooden chopping board or on the hob to protect your countertop. Use a spatula to lift the two halves onto two plates, then sandwich them together. Let it cool for a few minutes, but eat while the sandwich is still warm.

FOUR-FOLD PIZZA WRAPS

These four-fold wraps went viral a few years ago. My mum says she first saw them on YouTube Shorts though I'm not sure how, since she never watches YouTube. She claims it was for 'educational purposes', and maybe she's right because these wraps are genius.

This version is perfect when you need a quick pizza fix, but I also like to switch up the fillings. Try ham + cream cheese + lettuce + tomato or tuna + sweetcorn + rocket + mozzarella. If you've made the homemade pizza on page 140 and have any leftover toppings, you can use them again in this quick wrap. Or make a sweet version with sliced banana + chocolate spread + mini marshmallows + chopped nuts. With four sections to fill, the possibilities are endless.

Makes 2

½ red pepper

2 large flour tortilla wraps

50g grated Cheddar and mozzarella mix

3 tablespoons pesto rosso (page 82) or tomato sauce (page 46)

10 slices of pepperoni

1. Preheat your oven to 200°C for a conventional oven or 180°C for a fan oven.
2. Line a baking tray with non-stick baking paper.
3. Cut your red pepper into slices.
4. Put the tortillas on a chopping board. Using clean kitchen scissors, cut from the bottom edge of each tortilla up to the middle so that you have just one slit.
5. Divide your fillings in half, then put them in each of the four quadrants: sliced red pepper, cheese, pesto or tomato sauce, and pepperoni.
6. Starting with the bottom right quadrant, fold each tortilla up, then across, and finally down, creating a triangular pocket.
7. Put the folded wraps on the lined baking tray, then put the tray in the preheated oven and cook for 10 minutes, until the wraps are crispy and golden and the cheese has melted. Let them cool for a few minutes before tucking in.

QUICK CHICKEN RAMEN

Have you ever been so hungry after school that you start seeing visions of your favourite meals floating in front of you? Like you're in a game of Mario Kart, but instead of coins, it's steaming bowls of ramen just waiting to be devoured? All you can think about is opening your mouth and swallowing them whole. Ding ding ding! (That's the sound of me collecting stars for my noodles.)

This recipe is one of my favourites to cook because you can make it in minutes. I love coming home from school, kicking off my shoes and throwing my bag on the floor (I know, I know, I really need to work on that). I grab a saucepan, and in less than 10 minutes, I've got a real-life bowl of noodles right in front of me. Just hand me the chopsticks and it's time to start slurping. Ding ding ding…

Serves 1

100g cooked chicken slices

1 nest of dried egg noodles

25g frozen sweetcorn

25g frozen peas

½ chicken stock cube

1 tablespoon sour cream

1 tablespoon sesame oil

1 teaspoon soy sauce

2 spring onions or fresh chives

1. Use clean kitchen scissors to snip the cooked chicken slices into small pieces.

2. Put the noodles, corn and peas in a medium-sized saucepan. Pour in just enough water to cover the ingredients. Put the pan on a high heat on the hob and bring the water to a boil. When it's boiling, turn the heat down and let it simmer for about 6 minutes.

3. Carefully dunk a mug or measuring jug into the cooking water to save some (you need about 100ml), then carefully drain the noodles, corn and peas in a colander in the sink.

4. Put the noodles, corn and peas back in the saucepan and put the pan on a low heat. Crumble in half a chicken stock cube, then add the mug of cooking water and stir until the stock cube dissolves. Add the cooked chicken, sour cream, sesame oil and soy sauce and give everything one more stir.

5. Pour it all into your favourite bowl. Use clean kitchen scissors to snip the green tops of the spring onions or chives into small pieces straight over the top of the noodles, then slurp them up.

MEATBALL SUBS

With the perfect blend of herbs, these meatballs turn into flavour bombs. Stick those flavour bombs into a sub (which is a bread roll to you and me), smother them in tomato sauce and top it with melty cheese, and just like that, you've got the ultimate after-school feast. Or make a batch of the classic tomato sauce on page 46, cook a packet of spaghetti using the method on page 43 and put it all together to make spaghetti and meatballs.

Makes 4

For the meatballs:

500g beef mince (at least 8% fat)

50g Parmesan cheese

1 garlic clove

a few sprigs of fresh basil or 1 teaspoon dried basil

1 tablespoon dried oregano

1 teaspoon onion powder

¼ teaspoon dried chilli flakes

salt and pepper

For the subs:

4 hot dog rolls or mini baguettes

1 x 125g ball of fresh mozzarella

150g classic tomato sauce (page 46)

1. Preheat your oven to 200°C for a conventional oven or 180°C for a fan oven.

2. Line two baking trays with non-stick baking paper.

3. To make the meatballs, put the beef mince in a large mixing bowl and make a well in the centre.

4. Grate the Parmesan, then add it to the well. Peel the garlic, then grate it straight into the bowl.

5. Pick the basil leaves off the stems, then tear the leaves into the well (or add the dried basil if you're using that). Add the oregano, onion powder, chilli flakes and some salt and pepper, then mix everything together using your clean hands.

6. Divide the mixture into four equal portions, then divide each portion in three to make 12 portions in total. Roll each one into a ball, then put the meatballs on one of the lined baking trays.

7. Put the tray in the preheated oven and cook for 15 to 20 minutes, until the meatballs are fully cooked. To check, cut one in half to make sure there is no pink meat in the middle. If there is, put them back in the oven and cook for 5 more minutes, then check again.

8. Put your rolls or baguettes flat on your chopping board and put your hand on top to steady the bread. Use a serrated bread knife in a gentle sawing motion to cut each one horizontally through the centre, going all the way through. (Some hot dog rolls and mini baguettes come pre-sliced, so keep an eye out for those.) Put the split rolls on the second baking tray, cut sides facing up.

9. Tear the ball of mozzarella into pieces, then put one-quarter of the cheese on the top half of each roll. Spread some tomato sauce on the bottom half of each roll. Put the tray in the oven for the last 5 minutes of the meatballs' cooking time to warm the rolls and melt the cheese.

10 Using oven gloves, carefully remove the tray of meatballs and the tray of subs. Put one tray on a wooden chopping board and one tray on a clean tea towel to protect your countertop.

11 To serve, put three meatballs on the bottom half of each roll, then sandwich together with the top half.

SPEEDY MAC 'N' CHEESE

With only three ingredients this might not even look like a real recipe, but when you need a fast, fuss-free, cheesy pasta fix, it will be your go-to. It's the perfect comfort food when you're dealing with that after-school frazzle.

Serves 2

200g macaroni or penne

15g salted butter

100g grated Cheddar and mozzarella mix

salt and pepper

1. Cook your pasta using the method on page 43.

2. When the time is up, carefully dip a mug into the cooking water to save some of the pasta cooking water in case you need it for the sauce. Drain the pasta in a colander in the sink.

3. Put the pasta back in the saucepan and put the pan on a very low heat. Add the butter, stirring until it melts and coats the pasta. Gradually stir in the Cheddar and mozzarella until the cheese melts and forms a creamy sauce. If you want it to be a bit saucier, add a splash of the cooking water that you saved.

4. Sprinkle with a little salt and pepper, then serve immediately in two big bowls.

SPAGHETTI CARBONARA

I remember the day I first discovered comfort food. I was at the park, flying along on my skates, when I lost my balance and crashed into what I thought was long grass. Turns out it was a patch of nettles. To make matters worse, I was wearing shorts and a T-shirt, so I was covered from head to toe in painful, itchy stings. That day we found out that a bath with baking soda helps soothe nettle stings, but also that a bowl of spaghetti carbonara eases all pain.

Serves 4

200g Cheddar cheese

40g Parmesan cheese

2 garlic cloves

500g spaghetti

200g pancetta or bacon lardons

1 tablespoon olive oil

2 eggs

salt and pepper

1 bunch of fresh parsley

1. Preheat your oven to 200°C for a conventional oven or 180°C for a fan oven.
2. Grate the Cheddar and Parmesan cheese and keep them separate. Peel and grate the garlic.
3. Cook the spaghetti using the method on page 43.
4. While the pasta is cooking, put the pancetta or bacon lardons on a small baking tray. Add the grated garlic, then drizzle over the oil. Use your clean hands to toss together to coat the lardons in the garlic and oil.
5. Put the tray in the preheated oven and cook for 15 minutes, until the bacon is golden and sizzling. Using oven gloves, carefully remove the tray from the oven and put it on a wooden chopping board or on the hob to protect your countertop.
6. When the pasta is ready, carefully dip a mug into the cooking water to save some of it in case you need it for the sauce. Drain the spaghetti in a colander in the sink.
7. Crack the eggs into a large mixing bowl, then whisk them with a fork. Stir in all of the grated Cheddar and most of the grated Parmesan.
8. Using tongs, gradually add the hot spaghetti to the egg and cheese mixture to avoid scrambling the eggs.
9. Add the cooked bacon, then add a little salt and lots of black pepper. Gently mix for 5 minutes, until the eggs cook and the cheese melts. If the sauce is too thick or if the cheese needs a little help to get it to melt, add some of the hot pasta cooking water that you saved.
10. Finally, use clean kitchen scissors to snip the parsley into small pieces, then stir it into the pasta.
11. To serve, divide among four bowls, sprinkle the rest of the Parmesan on top and enjoy your comforting carbonara.

CRUNCHY PRAWN SPRING ROLLS

I love making these after school on a Friday to kick off the weekend. They're packed with prawns and crunchy veggies like carrots and bean sprouts (seriously, you have to try the bean sprouts). Just wait until you hear that satisfying crunch. Did I mention the crunch?

Makes 6

3 sheets of filo pastry

200g cooked, ready-to-eat prawns

1 carrot

1 garlic clove

1 teaspoon grated fresh ginger

4 spring onions or fresh chives

100g bean sprouts

1 tablespoon soy sauce, plus extra for dipping

1 tablespoon sweet chilli sauce, plus extra for dipping

1 tablespoon vegetable or olive oil

1 tablespoon sesame seeds (optional)

1. If your pastry is frozen, put it in the fridge overnight to thaw it. Put the frozen prawns in the fridge to thaw overnight too.

2. The next day, preheat your oven to 200°C for a conventional oven or 180°C for a fan oven.

3. Line a baking tray with non-stick baking paper.

4. Peel and grate the carrot, garlic and ginger. Put them in a large mixing bowl.

5. Use clean kitchen scissors to snip the green tops of the spring onions or chives into small pieces straight into the bowl.

6. Drain the ready-to-eat prawns in a colander in the sink to remove any extra water. Add them to the bowl along with the bean sprouts, soy sauce and sweet chilli sauce. Mix everything together with a wooden spoon.

7. Carefully unroll the filo sheets. Peel off the first sheet and lift it onto your clean countertop, then use clean kitchen scissors to cut it in half lengthways. Spoon a portion of the prawn mixture along the narrow edge of the sheet. Fold in the wide edges, then roll up tightly to form the spring roll. Put the roll on the lined baking tray, seam side down. Repeat with the rest of the filo sheets and filling.

8. Use a pastry brush to paint the tops of the rolls with a little oil, then sprinkle with sesame seeds (if using).

9. Put the tray in the preheated oven and cook for 20 minutes, until the rolls are golden and crisp.

10. Using oven gloves, carefully remove the tray from the oven and put it on a wooden chopping board or on the hob to protect your countertop. Let the rolls cool for a few minutes – there's nothing worse than burning your mouth because you were too impatient to wait!

11. Serve with little bowls of soy sauce and sweet chilli sauce on the side for dipping.

GOLDEN VEGGIE RICE

If you have leftover cooked rice, this is the perfect after-school food when you need a flavour hit and need it fast! But it's still easy to make even if you have to make the rice from scratch. The turmeric gives the rice its golden colour. With a few veggies thrown in for good measure, it will power you through homework.

Serves 4

1 cup basmati rice

2 cups water

1 small onion

1 garlic clove

2 carrots

2 tablespoons vegetable oil

1 tablespoon garam masala

1 teaspoon ground turmeric

50ml water

1 tablespoon tomato purée

50g frozen petits pois (peas)

50g frozen sweetcorn

salt and pepper

To garnish:

a handful of flaked almonds

a handful of fresh coriander or parsley leaves

1. Cook the rice using the recipe on page 30 (or this is a great way to use up leftover cooked rice – you need 250 grams of cooked rice for this recipe).

2. Peel and chop the onion. Peel and grate the garlic and carrots.

3. Put the oil in a large frying pan, then put the pan on the hob on a medium heat and let the oil warm up. Add the onion and garlic and cook for 3 minutes, until the onion is soft. Add the carrots and cook for 3 minutes, until the onion is golden.

4. Stir in the garam masala, turmeric and water. Cook for 1 minute to release their flavours, then stir in the tomato purée and cook for 2 or 3 minutes. Stir in the peas and sweetcorn and a little salt and pepper and cook for 2 minutes, until everything is heated through.

5. Add the cooked or leftover rice and mix everything together. Turn the heat down to low and cook for 5 minutes to bring all the flavours together. If you're using leftover cooked rice, you might need to let it cook for a little longer to reheat the rice until it's piping hot.

6. To serve, divide the rice among four bowls. Sprinkle over some flaked almonds and fresh coriander or parsley leaves as garnish. Tuck in and let every mouthful spur you on to help you finish your homework.

HAM AND CHEESE CROISSANTS

This is after-school fuel, coffee shop style! These ham and cheese croissants taste best when they're fresh out of the oven – perfect if you want to impress your friends when they come over for a play date. Serve them up, then sit back and wait for the compliments to roll in.

Makes 6

1 sheet of ready-rolled puff pastry

2 tablespoons mayonnaise

6 slice of cooked ham

6 slices of mature Cheddar cheese

1 egg

1. If your pastry is frozen, put it in the fridge overnight to thaw it.
2. The next day, preheat your oven to 200°C for a conventional oven or 180°C for a fan oven.
3. Line a baking tray with non-stick baking paper.
4. Unroll the puff pastry onto a large chopping board. Using a pizza cutter or a sharp knife, cut it into six triangles.
5. Spread a little mayonnaise on each pastry triangle, then top with a slice of ham and a slice of cheese.
6. Shape the croissants by starting at the wide end of each triangle, then roll the pastry towards the pointed tip to form a crescent shape. Put them on the lined baking tray.
7. Crack the egg into a small bowl, then whisk with a fork. Use a pastry brush to paint the top of each croissant with the beaten egg for a glossy, golden finish.
8. Put the tray in the preheated oven and bake for 20 minutes, until the croissants are puffed up and golden brown.
9. Using oven gloves, carefully remove the tray from the oven and put it on a wooden chopping board or on the hob to protect your countertop. Let the croissants cool on the tray for 5 minutes, then use a spatula to move them to a wire rack to finish cooling.

BAKE
ON
WON

STRAY SANDS AND POT-E=POT HOLDERS DERS

20-MINUTE FETA AND CHERRY TOMATO TAGLIATELLE TRAY BAKE

I have a confession: I'm not a fan of tomatoes. I always try to pick them out. But I love this recipe – it doesn't taste too tomatoey. The feta melts into the dish, making it super creamy. You can squash the tomatoes into the feta, creating a smooth sauce, and guess what? No need to pick them out! Whether you love or hate tomatoes, you'll love this.

Serves 4

4 tablespoons olive oil

200g feta cheese

500g cherry tomatoes on the vine

2 garlic cloves

a little pepper

500g tagliatelle

To garnish:

a few sprigs of fresh basil

1. Preheat your oven to 200°C for a conventional oven or 180°C for a fan oven.

2. Drizzle 2 tablespoons of the oil into a large rectangular baking dish or a wide, shallow casserole.

3. Put the whole block of feta in the middle of the dish and scatter the cherry tomatoes around it. You can keep them on the vines to make it look fancy.

4. Peel the garlic cloves, then grate them straight into the dish (or you can slice them if you want to level up). Drizzle with the remaining 2 tablespoons of olive oil and add a good amount of black pepper. You don't need to use any salt because the feta is already salty.

5. Put the dish in the preheated oven and bake for 20 minutes.

6. Meanwhile, cook the pasta using the method on page 43.

7. When the time is up, carefully dip a mug into the cooking water to save some of it in case you want to thin down the sauce. Drain the pasta in a colander in the sink.

8. Using oven gloves, carefully remove the baking dish from the oven and put it on a wooden chopping board or on the hob to protect your countertop. Add the cooked tagliatelle. Using tongs, mix everything together until the pasta is coated in the creamy sauce. If you think the sauce is too thick, add some of the pasta cooking water that you saved and stir it in.

9. To serve, put a potholder or clean tea towel in the middle of the table and put the dish on top. Pick the leaves off the basil sprigs, then tear them over the top of the pasta. Let everyone dig in and help themselves.

CHICKEN FAJITA TRAY BAKE

This tray bake always gets a big thumbs-up in our kids' cooking classes. You can build your fajitas however you like, but try not to skip the onions and peppers. The different flavours will make your fajitas taste epic. Be brave and give them a try. If you don't, you'll never know how good they are. Your taste-buddies will thank you for it.

Serves 4

1 red pepper

1 green pepper

1 yellow pepper

1 red onion

1 garlic clove

8 fresh chives

4 chicken fillets

For the spice paste:

1 tablespoon olive oil

2 teaspoons dried oregano

2 teaspoons smoked paprika

1 teaspoon ground cumin

a pinch of cayenne pepper (optional)

salt and pepper

1. Preheat your oven to 200°C for a conventional oven or 180°C for a fan oven.

2. Line two large baking trays with non-stick baking paper.

3. Slice the peppers and onion. Peel and grate the garlic. Use clean kitchen scissors to snip the chives into small pieces, then put them in a small bowl and save them for later.

4. Use your scissors again to cut the chicken fillets into strips 2cm wide.

5. Put all the spice paste ingredients in a large bowl and mix together. Add the peppers, onions, garlic and chicken. Mix everything together using clean hands, making sure everything is coated in the paste. Divide the mixture evenly between the two lined baking trays, then wash your hands with warm soapy water.

6. Put the trays in the preheated oven and cook for 30 minutes, until the chicken is fully cooked and the peppers and onions are soft. (Read the tips on page 10 about how to check that the chicken is cooked.)

7. To warm the tortillas, tear off a large sheet of foil. Stack the tortillas on top of each other, then wrap them in the foil. Put them on the lower shelf of the oven during the last 5 minutes of the cooking time for the chicken and veg.

8. When the chicken and veg are cooked, use oven gloves to carefully remove the trays from the oven and put them on a wooden chopping board or on the hob to protect your countertop. Sprinkle the fresh chives directly over the trays. Unwrap the warmed tortillas and put them on a plate.

9. Cut the limes into wedges, then put them in a small serving bowl or on the trays. Put the grated cheese in a serving bowl too.

To serve:

8 to 12 flour tortillas

2 limes

200g grated Cheddar and mozzarella mix

1 small tub of crème fraîche or sour cream

chilli flakes (optional)

10. Put two potholders or clean tea towels in the middle of the table and put the trays on top. Bring the tortillas, lime wedges, grated cheese, the tub of crème fraîche or sour cream and the spice jar of chilli flakes to the table.

11. Make your fajita by putting a warm tortilla on your plate. Add some of the chicken, peppers and onions in the middle, then top with a spoonful of crème fraîche or sour cream, a squeeze of lime and a pinch of chilli flakes if you're feeling brave. Finally, scatter over some grated cheese.

12. Fold in the sides of the tortilla so nothing falls out (if your dog is like ours, it will be licking its chops at this point, hoping a little piece will drop onto the floor). Starting from the bottom and keeping the sides tucked in, roll it up tightly and tuck in!

SPICE BAG TRAY BAKE

If you're Irish, you'll know all about the legendary spice bag. But if you're not from Ireland, let me give you a quick rundown. A spice bag is a magical combination of chips, crispy chicken and veg, all tossed in a secret blend of spices and served in a paper bag in takeaways. The spice mix is what makes it so epic.

Serves 4

2 or 3 large Maris Piper potatoes
2 tablespoons olive oil
2 red peppers
2 green peppers
2 white onions

For the spice mix:

1 tablespoon Chinese five-spice powder
1 teaspoon garlic powder
1 teaspoon paprika
1 teaspoon ground ginger
1 teaspoon light brown sugar
1 teaspoon salt
½ teaspoon ground white pepper
a pinch of cayenne pepper (optional)

1. Preheat your oven to 200°C for a conventional oven or 180°C for a fan oven.
2. Line two large baking trays with non-stick baking paper.
3. To make the spice mix, put all the spices in a small bowl and mix together.
4. Wash the potatoes and leave the skins on. Cut them in half, then slice them into thick rectangular chips. Rinse the chips in a colander under cold running water for 1 minute to remove the starch – this will give you crispier chips.
5. Pat the chips dry with kitchen paper, then put them on one of the lined baking trays. Drizzle with 1 tablespoon of oil, then add a pinch of the spice mix. Use your clean hands to toss together until all the chips are coated in oil and spices.
6. Cut the peppers and onions into slices.
7. Put the peppers and onions on one half of the second lined tray, then drizzle with 1 tablespoon of oil and sprinkle over the rest of the spice mix. Use your clean hands to toss everything together to coat the veg in the oil and spices.
8. To prepare the chicken, use clean kitchen scissors to cut the chicken fillets into strips 2cm wide. Put the strips on a plate.
9. Get two wide, shallow bowls. Put the ground almonds, paprika, salt and pepper in the first bowl and mix them together.
10. Crack the eggs into the second bowl, then whisk them with a fork.
11. Working with one chicken strip at a time, dip it into the beaten eggs, then into the ground almond mix, making sure it's completely coated. Put the coated chicken on the tray with the peppers and onions. Repeat with the rest of the chicken.

For the crispy chicken:

3 chicken fillets

170g ground almonds

1 teaspoon paprika

½ teaspoon salt

½ teaspoon pepper

2 eggs

To serve:

a few sprigs of fresh coriander

satay sauce (page 152)

12. Put both trays in the preheated oven and cook for 40 minutes, until the chicken is fully cooked (see page 10), the peppers and onions are soft and the chips are golden brown.

13. To serve, put two potholders or clean tea towels in the middle of the table and put the trays on top. Pick the coriander leaves off the stems and scatter them over the trays. Put a bowl of satay sauce on the side and let everyone dig in and help themselves, but serve yourself before your siblings or they will devour it all!

ONE-POT LEMON PEPPER CHICKEN DRUMSTICKS WITH RICE

This dish is sure to impress the whole family, so save it for when your granny comes to visit. You've got chicken drumsticks tossed in a homemade lemon pepper seasoning, veggies and rice, all cooked in one pot. And you know how grannies are when they're proud of you – you might just find a sneaky fiver slipped your way. Cha-ching!

Serves 4

300g easy-cook long-grain rice

1 red pepper

1 green pepper

1 yellow pepper

1 tablespoon olive oil

350ml chicken stock

200ml cream

8 chicken drumsticks

For the lemon pepper seasoning:

1 lemon

1 teaspoon garlic powder

1 teaspoon onion powder

1 teaspoon ground white pepper

3 tablespoons olive oil

1. Preheat your oven to 200°C for a conventional oven or 180°C for a fan oven.

2. To make the lemon pepper seasoning, zest the lemon (page 19). Put the lemon zest in a small bowl with the garlic and onion powders and ground white pepper and mix together, then stir in the oil to create a thick paste.

3. Cut the lemon into four or six wedges. Put them on a plate for later.

4. Put the rice in a fine mesh sieve and rinse it under cold running water from the tap until the water runs clear. This will prevent it from sticking together.

5. Cut the peppers into slices.

6. Drizzle the oil into a large baking dish or a large, shallow casserole. Add the rice and peppers, then pour in the chicken stock and cream and mix it all together.

7. Use a pastry brush to paint the chicken drumsticks with the lemon pepper seasoning, then put them on top of the rice and peppers. Pour any leftover seasoning over the top.

8. Cover the dish with foil or cover the casserole with a lid. Put it in the preheated oven and cook for 50 minutes, until the rice has absorbed all the stock and the chicken is cooked. (Read the tips on page 10 about how to check that the chicken is cooked.)

9. Using oven gloves, carefully remove the dish from the oven and put it on a wooden chopping board or on the hob to protect your countertop. Remove the foil or lid, then put the dish back in the oven. Cook for 10 more minutes, until the skin on the drumsticks is golden brown.

To garnish:

a few sprigs of fresh parsley

10 Use your oven gloves again to remove the dish from the oven and put it back on the chopping board or hob. Remove the drumsticks using tongs and put them on a plate.

11 Finish by squeezing in the juice from one of the lemon wedges. Use a fork to stir it in while also fluffing up the rice at the same time.

12 Put the drumsticks back in the dish or casserole, then use clean kitchen scissors to snip the parsley into small pieces straight over the top to garnish.

13 To serve, put a potholder or clean tea towel in the middle of the table and put the dish or casserole on top. Wrap a clean tea towel around the dish or casserole to remind everyone that it's hot. Put the rest of the lemon wedges in a bowl if anyone wants to squeeze over a little extra juice.

FANCY FISH 'N' CHIPS

We're getting fancy with our fish 'n' chips! The fresh herbs and homemade tartar sauce take this tray bake to a whole new level. Get ready for some seriously posh nosh.

Serves 4

For the fish:

1 lemon

30g Parmesan cheese

2 eggs

50g panko breadcrumbs

4 x 125g white fish fillets, skinned and boned (ask the fishmonger to do this for you)

For the chips:

6 large Maris Piper potatoes

2 tablespoons olive oil

salt and pepper

For the tartar sauce:

6 tablespoons mayonnaise

2 small gherkins

1 tablespoon capers

a few sprigs of fresh dill or 1 teaspoon dried dill

1. Preheat your oven to 220°C for a conventional oven or 200°C for a fan oven.
2. Line two large baking trays with non-stick baking paper.
3. Peel the potatoes and cut them in half, then cut them into rectangular chips. Rinse the chips in a colander under cold running water for 1 minute to remove the starch – this will give you crispier chips. Pat them dry with kitchen paper.
4. Drizzle the oil on one of the lined baking trays, then add the chips, sprinkle with a little salt and pepper and use your clean hands to toss the chips to coat them in the oil. Put the tray in the preheated oven and set a timer for 25 minutes.
5. Meanwhile, zest the lemon (page 19), then cut the lemon into six wedges. Grate the Parmesan cheese.
6. Get two wide, shallow bowls. Crack the eggs into the first bowl, then squeeze in the juice from one lemon wedge and whisk with a fork.
7. Put the lemon zest in the second bowl with the panko breadcrumbs, grated Parmesan and a little salt and pepper and mix together.
8. Dip each fish fillet into the eggs, then dip it into the breadcrumb mixture, making sure it's completely coated. If you have any breadcrumb mixture left over, you could give the fish a second coating in the egg and breadcrumbs to make it even crispier. Put all the breaded fish on the second lined tray.
9. When the timer goes off after the chips have been cooking for 25 minutes, put the tray of fish in the oven too and cook for 15 minutes more.
10. To make the tartar sauce, put the mayonnaise in a small bowl.
11. Slice the gherkins, then chop them using the scatter or mezzaluna method on page 23. Add them to the mayo.

12 Put the capers in a fine mesh sieve and rinse them under cold running water, then tip them out onto a chopping board. Mash them with a fork, then stir them into the mayo.

13 Use clean kitchen scissors to snip the fresh dill into small pieces straight into the mayo or add the dried dill. Squeeze in the juice from one of the lemon wedges. Stir everything together.

14 Serve the fish 'n' chips with the rest of the lemon wedges and a small bowl of tartar sauce on the side.

STICKY SALMON TRAY BAKE

This speedy tray bakes takes only 15 minutes to cook. The noodles taste so good straight from the bowl that it's hard not to eat them all, so be warned!

Serves 4

1 yellow pepper
1 green pepper
1 red pepper
1 garlic clove
1 teaspoon grated ginger
4 spring onions
4 salmon fillets
4 tablespoons sweet chilli sauce
150g cashews

For the noodles:

4 nests of dried egg noodles
2 tablespoons sesame oil
8 tablespoons water
2 tablespoons soy sauce
2 tablespoons oyster sauce
2 tablespoons sweet chilli sauce
2 tablespoons honey

1. Preheat your oven to 200°C for a conventional oven or 180°C for a fan oven.

2. Line a large baking tray with non-stick baking paper.

3. Cut the peppers into slices, then put them on the lined baking tray. Peel and grate the garlic and ginger, then scatter them over the peppers and toss together.

4. Use clean kitchen scissors to snip the green tops of the spring onions into small pieces. Put them in a small bowl to use later. Snip the white part of the spring onions into small pieces directly over the tray of peppers and toss to combine.

5. Put the salmon on top of the veggies. Use a pastry brush to paint the top of each fillet with 1 tablespoon of sweet chilli sauce.

6. Put the tray in the preheated oven and cook for 5 minutes to soften the veggies slightly. When the time is up, use oven gloves to carefully remove the baking tray from the oven and put it on a wooden chopping board or on the hob to protect your countertop.

7. Scatter the cashew nuts over the top and put the tray back in the oven. Cook for another 15 minutes, until the salmon is cooked through. To check that the salmon is cooked, use a fork to gently press on the thickest part of the salmon. If the fish flakes apart easily and looks solid in colour rather than shiny or see-through, it's ready. If it's not, put the tray back in the oven and cook for 5 more minutes.

8. While the salmon is cooking, fill your kettle with water and boil it. Put the noodles in a saucepan, pour over the just-boiled water, cover the pan with a lid and let them soak for 4 minutes, until soft.

9. After 4 minutes, drain the noodles in a colander in a sink, then put them back in the pan. Drizzle with the sesame oil, then use tongs to toss the noodles in the oil so they don't stick together.

10. Add the water, soy sauce, oyster sauce, sweet chilli sauce and honey. Mix everything together to coat the noodles in the sauce.

11 To dish up, divide the salmon, veg and noodles among four serving bowls or plates, then sprinkle over the spring onion tops. Serve while it's still steaming hot and enjoy slurping up the noodles.

SAUSAGE AND APPLE TRAY BAKE WITH SWEET POTATO CURLS

The flavour combos on this tray are next level. Once you nail these sweet potato curls, you'll be whipping them up for every family movie night from here on out. Trust me, they really are that good. If you have any posh beans from page 65 left over, we like to have them with this tray bake.

Serves 4

2 large sweet potatoes

1 red pepper

1 green pepper

1 red onion

2 garlic cloves

2 red apples

8 large pork sausages

2 tablespoons olive oil

1 teaspoon dried sage

salt and pepper

4 vacuum-packed mini corncobs

To garnish:

a few sprigs of fresh parsley

1. Preheat your oven to 200°C for a conventional oven or 180°C for a fan oven.

2. Line two large baking trays with non-stick baking paper.

3. Peel the sweet potatoes using a vegetable peeler and throw away those first peelings. Now continue to peel each one into thin strips with the peeler.

4. Slice the peppers and onion. Peel and grate the garlic. Peel and core the apples, then cut them into wedges. Use clean kitchen scissors to snip the parsley into small pieces.

5. Divide the sweet potatoes, peppers, onion, garlic, apples and sausages between the two lined trays. Drizzle with the oil and sprinkle over the sage and a little salt and pepper. Mix everything together with your clean hands, making sure all the ingredients are coated with oil.

6. Put the trays in the preheated oven and cook for 15 minutes.

7. Using oven gloves, carefully remove the trays from the oven and put them on a wooden chopping board or on the hob to protect your countertop. Using a spatula, turn over the veg, apples and sausages, then put the trays back in the oven and cook for 15 more minutes.

8. Take the trays out of the oven again and add the corn. Put the trays back in the oven to cook for a final 10 minutes.

9. To serve, put two potholders or clean tea towels in the middle of the table and put the trays on top to let everyone help themselves. Garnish with the fresh parsley and dig in!

ONE-POT SWEDISH MEATBALLS

This is one of my dad's Friday-night favourites. Every time I cook it, he still asks, 'Did you really make this?' I always tell him it's so easy to make, even dads can do it. He then says, 'But you do it so much better.' I'm not sure if that's true or if he's just getting out of making dinner again.

Serves 4

500g beef mince (look for mince with 5% fat so the dish won't be too oily)

2 garlic cloves

1 teaspoon Worcestershire sauce

salt and pepper

200g chestnut mushrooms

200g easy-cook long-grain rice

1 tablespoon olive oil

350ml beef stock

100ml cream

1 teaspoon cranberry sauce, plus extra to serve

½ teaspoon dried sage

To serve:

a few sprigs of fresh parsley

freshly grated Parmesan cheese

1. Preheat your oven to 200°C for a conventional oven or 180°C for a fan oven.

2. Put the beef mince in a large mixing bowl. Peel the garlic, then grate it straight into the bowl. Add the Worcestershire sauce and a little salt and pepper. Mix together using your clean hands, then roll into 12 meatballs. Put them on a plate.

3. Slice the mushrooms.

4. Put the rice in a fine mesh sieve and rinse it under cold running water from the tap until the water runs clear. This will prevent it from sticking together.

5. Drizzle the oil in the bottom of a casserole. Add the rice and mushrooms. Pour in the beef stock and cream, then stir in the cranberry sauce, sage and a little salt and pepper. Put the meatballs on top of the rice mixture.

6. Cover the casserole with a lid, put it in the preheated oven and cook for 1 hour.

7. Use clean kitchen scissors to snip the parsley into small pieces.

8. Grate enough Parmesan cheese to sprinkle some over each portion.

9. Put a potholder or clean tea towel in the middle of the table and put the casserole on top. Scatter over the parsley, then serve straight from the dish with a good sprinkling of freshly grated Parmesan and some extra cranberry sauce on the side.

DOUBLE CHEESE, DOUBLE BURGER

There's only one thing better than a cheeseburger, and that's a double cheeseburger. This is how you reach legendary status – or rather, double legend.

Makes 4 double burgers

400g beef mince

400g pork mince

2 garlic cloves

1 tablespoon Worcestershire sauce

1 teaspoon onion powder

1 teaspoon paprika

salt and pepper

8 slices of cheese

For the caramelised onions:

2 large red onions

2 tablespoons olive oil

1 tablespoon honey

1. Preheat your oven to 200°C for a conventional oven or 180°C for a fan oven.

2. Line a baking tray with non-stick baking paper.

3. Put the beef and pork mince in a large mixing bowl. Peel the garlic, then grate it straight into the bowl. Add the Worcestershire sauce, onion powder, paprika and a little salt and pepper.

4. Mix everything together with your clean hands. Divide the mixture into eight equal portions, then roll each one into a ball. Flatten each ball into a patty, making each one a little bigger than the size of your burger buns because the burgers will shrink when they cook. Put all the burgers on one side of the lined baking tray.

5. Cut the onions into slices. Put them on the tray next to the burgers, then drizzle the onions with the oil and honey and toss to coat them in the oil.

6. Put the tray in the preheated oven and cook for 17 minutes. Using oven gloves, carefully remove the tray from the oven and put it on a wooden chopping board or on the hob to protect your countertop. Put a slice of cheese on top of each burger. Pop the tray back in the oven for 3 minutes to melt the cheese.

7. Put the burger buns on a baking tray, cut sides facing up. Put them in the oven at the same time that you put the burgers back in and toast for 3 minutes.

8. To make the burger sauce, put the mayo, ketchup, mustard and pickle brine in a small bowl and stir together.

9. To assemble, spread the bottom half of each bun with burger sauce. Add one cheeseburger, then pile some caramelised red onions on top. Put another cheeseburger on top and add more red onions, then sandwich together with the top half of the bun. Serve with a big handful of your favourite crisps on the side.

For the burger sauce:

4 tablespoons mayonnaise

2 tablespoons ketchup

1 tablespoon Dijon mustard

1 tablespoon brine from a jar of pickles

To serve:

4 burger buns

your favourite crisps

KOFTA TRAY BAKE

A kofta is like a Middle Eastern and Indian version of a meatball. We're grating an onion for these koftas, so prepare for the waterworks and have your onion goggles at the ready! Grating the onion makes the meatballs super juicy. Trust me, the tears are worth it.

Serves 4

For the koftas:

500g lamb or beef mince

50g fresh breadcrumbs

1 egg

1 teaspoon curry powder

salt and pepper

½ onion

For the tray bake:

½ onion

1 green pepper

1 large Maris Piper potato

12 cherry tomatoes

2 tablespoons olive oil

4 pittas

50g flaked almonds

1 x 200g block of feta cheese

1 x 100g pack of pomegranate seeds

1. Preheat your oven to 200°C for a conventional oven or 180°C for a fan oven.

2. To make the seasoning mix, put all the ingredients in a small bowl and stir everything together.

3. Put the lamb or beef mince and breadcrumbs in a large mixing bowl. Crack in the egg, then add the curry powder and a little salt and pepper.

4. Put on your onion goggles (page 17), then peel the onion and cut it in half. Set one half aside for the tray bake. Grate the other half on the large holes of a box grater. Add the grated onion to the bowl.

5. Mix everything together with clean hands. Shape the mixture into 12 meatballs. Divide them between two large baking trays.

6. Cut the other onion half into slices. Slice the green pepper. Scatter the onion and pepper around the meatballs on the baking trays.

7. Peel the potato, then cut it in half lengthways. Now cut the halves into wedges, then cut the wedges into cubes. Add the potato cubes and the whole cherry tomatoes to the trays.

8. Drizzle the oil over everything, then scatter over the seasoning mix. Use your hands to gently toss everything together to coat in the oil and spices.

9. Put the trays in the preheated oven and cook for 40 minutes.

10. Use clean kitchen scissors to cut each pitta in half, then pop them into your toaster on a low heat to gently warm them up.

11. Using oven gloves, carefully remove the trays from the oven and put them on a wooden chopping board or on the hob to protect your countertop. Scatter over the flaked almonds. Pop both trays back in the oven for 5 minutes, until the almonds are lightly toasted.

For the seasoning mix:

1 teaspoon dried oregano

1 teaspoon dried thyme

1 teaspoon dried basil

1 teaspoon garlic powder

1 teaspoon onion powder

To serve:

shop-bought hummus or tzatziki

12 Remove the trays from the oven and put them on the wooden chopping board or hob. Crumble over the feta cheese, then scatter over the pomegranate seeds.

13 To serve, put two potholders or clean tea towels in the middle of the table and put the trays on top. Serve the toasted pittas and bowls of hummus or tzatziki on the side and let everyone dig in and help themselves.

PIZZA NIGHT

I love making pizza from scratch for lots of reasons. When I'm kneading the dough, any worries I have just seem to melt away into it. Plus a homemade pizza can be any shape you want. That's how you know it's homemade, right? Another bonus is that this pizza doesn't take forever. There's no waiting around for the dough to rise, so you get to enjoy your hard work almost instantly. What kid likes waiting for anything anyway? But the thing I love most is that there are no rules. You can put whatever you like on your pizza, even ham and pineapple if that's your thing. And let's be real, who needs veggies when it's pizza night?

Makes 1 large pizza

For the dough:

200g plain flour, plus extra for the countertop

1 x 7g sachet of fast-action dried yeast

1 teaspoon salt

120ml lukewarm water

2 tablespoons olive oil

For the quick tomato sauce (or use some classic tomato sauce on page 46):

2 tablespoons tomato purée

1 teaspoon dried oregano

1 teaspoon caster sugar

1. Preheat your oven to 240°C. It doesn't matter if you're using a conventional or a fan oven, you want the temperature to be as high as it can go.

2. For this pizza, you can use a pizza pan or a regular baking tray. Just make sure to line the pan or tray with non-stick baking paper so the pizza doesn't stick to it.

3. To make the dough, put the flour, yeast and salt in a large mixing bowl and stir together. Make a well in the centre.

4. Pour the warm water and oil into the well and mix everything together with a wooden spoon until it starts to come together into a dough.

5. Sprinkle a little flour on your clean countertop, then tip the dough out onto it. Put a little flour on your hands. Bring the dough together into a ball, then press it down and fold it in onto itself. Keep pressing and folding for at least 5 minutes, until you have a nice smooth dough.

6. Roll out your dough into whatever shape you like (my mum always says the more rustic, the better), then put it on your lined pizza pan or baking tray.

7. Make the quick tomato sauce by mixing the tomato purée, oregano and sugar together in a small bowl. Spread the sauce evenly over the dough, but keep a 1cm rim clear around the edges for the crust. Sprinkle the cheese on top, then add your favourite toppings.

8. When your pizza is ready to go into the oven, reduce the temperature to 200°C for a conventional oven or 180°C for a fan oven.

Toppings:

100g grated Cheddar and mozzarella mix

a selection of your favourites, such as pepperoni, salami, sweetcorn, red pepper, ham, pineapple

a few fresh basil leaves

9. Put the tray in the preheated oven and cook for 20 to 30 minutes, until the pizza crust is golden and the cheese is melted and bubbling.

10. Using oven gloves, carefully remove the tray from the oven and put it on a wooden chopping board or on the hob to protect your countertop. Scatter over a few fresh basil leaves when it comes out of the oven.

11. Let the pizza sit for 5 minutes, then use a spatula to slide it off the tray and onto the chopping board. Use a pizza cutter to cut it into slices and enjoy – it will be on the table faster than delivery.

CHEESY GARLIC FLATBREAD

This flatbread brushed with garlic butter and loaded with melty mozzarella is the ultimate sidekick for a weekend pizza night (page 140), but it's also perfect to snack on by itself, dunked into the classic tomato sauce on page 46.

Makes 1 large flatbread for sharing

200g plain flour, plus extra for the countertop

1 teaspoon baking powder

a pinch of salt

200g natural Greek yogurt

1 tablespoon milk, if needed

1 tablespoon olive oil

For the garlic butter:

50g salted butter

1 garlic clove

a few sprigs of fresh parsley

For the topping:

1 x 125g ball of fresh mozzarella

1 The butter needs to be soft to make the garlic butter, so take it out of the fridge at least 2 hours before you start to cook.

2 Preheat your oven to 200°C for a conventional oven or 180°C for a fan oven.

3 Line a baking tray with non-stick baking paper.

4 To make the flatbread, put the flour, baking powder and salt in a large mixing bowl and stir together. Add the yogurt and stir with a wooden spoon until it starts to come together into a dough. If the dough is too dry and isn't coming together, add the milk. Now use your clean hands to shape it into a ball, then drizzle it with the oil. Cover the bowl with a clean tea towel and let the dough rest while you make the garlic butter.

5 Put the soft butter in a medium-sized mixing bowl. If you've forgotten to take it out of the fridge, don't worry! You can grate the cold butter using the large holes on a box grater instead to make it easy to mix. Put it in a bowl and mash it with a fork until it's smooth.

6 Peel the garlic, then grate it straight into the bowl with the butter. Use clean kitchen scissors to snip the parsley into small pieces straight into the bowl, then mix it all together with the fork.

7 Open the packet or tub of fresh mozzarella over the sink to drain off the liquid it comes in. Tear the ball into pieces with your hands, then put the cheese on a plate.

8 Sprinkle your clean countertop with a little flour, then tip the ball of dough onto it. Roll it out into whatever shape you like, but it should be about 1cm thick.

9 Put the flatbread on the lined baking tray. Use a butter knife to spread the garlic butter all over the flatbread, then scatter the torn mozzarella all over.

10 Put the tray in the preheated oven and bake for 30 minutes, until the flatbread is golden brown and the cheese is melted and bubbling.

11 Using oven gloves, carefully remove the tray from the oven and put it on a wooden chopping board or on the hob to protect your countertop.

12 Serve alongside the pizza on page 140 or cut it into fingers for dipping into the tomato sauce on page 46.

MOVIE NIGHT NACHOS

We like to keep our movie night nachos simple. We bring the spice, but not too much. The cheese sauce is a star on its own, and the guac is super creamy. Just try not to devour them all before you've even picked a movie.

Serves 4

8 flour tortilla wraps

2 tablespoons olive oil

1 teaspoon smoked paprika

salt and pepper

For the cheese sauce:

200g Cheddar cheese (or a mix of Cheddar and mozzarella)

1 x 410g tin of evaporated milk

1 teaspoon cornflour

For the salsa:

3 large, ripe tomatoes

1 small red onion

½ lime

1 bunch of fresh coriander or parsley

1. Preheat your oven to 200°C for a conventional oven or 180°C for a fan oven.

2. Using clean kitchen scissors, cut the tortilla wraps into triangles. Divide them between two large baking trays and drizzle with the oil. Sprinkle over the smoked paprika and a little salt and pepper, then use your clean hands to toss the tortilla pieces to coat them all in the oil. Spread the pieces out evenly on the trays.

3. Put the trays in the preheated oven and cook for 8 minutes, until the tortillas are nice and crispy.

4. Using oven gloves, carefully remove the trays from the oven and put them on a wooden chopping board or on the hob to protect your countertop. Let the tortilla chips cool and harden.

5. To make the cheese sauce, grate the cheese. Put it in a saucepan and stir in the evaporated milk and cornflour. Put the pan on a low heat on the hob. Stir now and then until the cheese melts into a silky sauce.

6. To make the salsa, cut the tomatoes in half, then scoop out the seeds with a small spoon. Cut the tomatoes into small pieces and put them in a mixing bowl.

7. Peel the red onion, then chop it into small pieces and add it to the bowl.

8. Cut a lime in half. Squeeze the juice of half of the lime over the tomatoes and onion. Save the other half for the guacamole. Using your scissors again, snip the fresh coriander or parsley into small pieces straight into the bowl. Add a little salt and pepper and mix together.

For the guacamole:

2 ripe avocados

1 teaspoon garlic powder

¼ teaspoon chilli flakes

½ lime

9. To make the guacamole, cut the avocados in half lengthways. Twist the avocados to separate the halves, then remove the stone with a spoon. Use the spoon to scoop out the flesh into a bowl, then mash it with a fork or potato masher. Add the garlic powder, chilli flakes and the juice of the other half of the lime. Add a little salt and pepper, then stir it all together.

10. Serve the homemade tortilla chips with the cheese sauce, salsa and guacamole in separate bowls for dipping.

OVEN-BAKED DUMPLINGS

I'm obsessed with dumplings, and I couldn't believe how easy and fun they are to make at home. You can even make the wrappers from scratch. They're perfect for a play date with your bestie – you'll have a blast making them together and trying to nail that crescent moon shape. But you can also buy ready-made frozen wrappers in Asian food stores if you want to take a shortcut.

Dumplings are usually fried and steamed in a pan, but I'll be honest, that can be tricky, so we bake them instead. They look super impressive and taste absolutely unreal.

Makes 12

For the dough:

200g plain flour

120ml lukewarm water

1 tablespoon cornflour

For the filling:

1 small carrot

2 spring onions or fresh chives

1 garlic clove

200g pork mince

20g sweetcorn

1 tablespoon soy sauce, plus extra for dipping

1 tablespoon honey

1 teaspoon Chinese five-spice powder

½ teaspoon ground ginger

1 tablespoon vegetable oil

1. To make the dough, put the flour in a large mixing bowl. Make a well in the centre, then pour in the warm water. Use chopsticks or a wooden spoon to stir until it comes together into a dough.

2. Sprinkle your clean countertop, your hands and the dough with the cornflour. Tip the dough onto the counter. Bring the dough together into a ball, then press it down and fold it in onto itself. Keep pressing and folding for a couple of minutes, until you have a smooth dough. Use your hands to roll the dough into a log 16cm long, then wrap it in cling film and put it in the fridge while you make the filling.

3. Peel the carrot and grate it using the large holes of a box grater, then put it in a large mixing bowl. Use clean kitchen scissors to snip the green tops of the spring onions or chives into small pieces straight into the bowl. Peel the garlic, then grate it straight into the bowl too.

4. Put the pork mince, sweetcorn, soy sauce, honey, Chinese five-spice powder and ginger in the bowl. Use your clean hands to mix everything together really well.

5. Preheat your oven to 200°C for a conventional oven or 180°C for a fan oven.

6. Line a baking tray with non-stick baking paper.

7. Take the dough out of the fridge and remove the cling film. Cut it into 12 slices.

8. Flatten each piece of dough with your hand, then use a rolling pin to roll it out into a circle about 10cm in diameter. If the dough is sticking to the rolling pin or your countertop, sprinkle it with a little cornflour. Use an 8cm scone cutter or cookie cutter to stamp out each circle of dough into a perfect round.

9   Fill a small bowl with water and put it next to you. Working with one wrapper at a time, put 1 teaspoon of filling in the middle. It might not seem like very much, but resist the temptation to add more filling, otherwise the dumplings might burst open during cooking.

10 Dip your finger in the water and run it around the edge of the wrapper. Fold the wrapper in half so that it forms a half-moon shape, then pinch the edges together. Make sure the edges are completely sealed to keep the filling inside. Put the dumplings on the lined baking tray and repeat with the rest of the wrappers and filling. (If you want to level up, search for dumpling folding tutorials on YouTube, there are lots of helpful videos to make pleats and different shapes.)

11 Use a pastry brush to paint the top of each dumpling with a little oil. Put the tray in the preheated oven and cook for 25 to 30 minutes, until the dumplings are golden brown.

12 Using oven gloves, carefully remove the tray from the oven and put it on a wooden chopping board or on the hob to protect your countertop. Let the dumplings cool for a few minutes.

13 Serve the dumplings with a small bowl of soy sauce on the side for dipping.

CRISPY CHICKEN GOUJONS WITH SECRET SAUCE

These oven-baked chicken goujons plus our creamy, tangy, secret sauce are the ultimate homemade treat.

Serves 4

4 large chicken fillets
200g plain flour
1 teaspoon paprika
½ teaspoon garlic powder
1 teaspoon salt
1 teaspoon ground white pepper
3 eggs
200g panko breadcrumbs
2 tablespoons olive oil

For the secret sauce:

8 tablespoons mayonnaise
4 tablespoons ketchup
½ teaspoon garlic powder
½ teaspoon smoked paprika
½ teaspoon ground white pepper
½ teaspoon Worcestershire sauce
¼ teaspoon salt

1. To make the sauce, put all the ingredients in a bowl and mix together. Put the bowl in the fridge for at least 30 minutes, but 1 hour is better for the best flavour.

2. Preheat your oven to 200°C for a conventional oven or 180°C for a fan oven.

3. Line a baking tray with non-stick baking paper.

4. Using clean kitchen scissors, cut your chicken into strips the size of an adult's finger (maybe that's why it's called finger food?).

5. To set up your breading station, you need three bowls. Put the flour, paprika, garlic powder, salt and white pepper in one bowl and mix together. Crack the eggs into the second bowl, then whisk with a fork. Put the breadcrumbs in the third bowl. Line up the bowls in a row: flour first, then eggs, then breadcrumbs.

6. Dip each piece of chicken into the flour first, then the eggs, then the breadcrumbs, making sure it's completely coated in breadcrumbs. Put the breaded goujon on the lined tray. Repeat with the remaining chicken strips.

7. If you have any breading mixture left over, you could give some of the goujons a second coating in the flour, eggs and breadcrumbs to make them even crispier. When all the goujons have been breaded, make sure they are in a single layer on the tray, then drizzle over the oil. This will help to make them crispy.

8. Put the tray in the preheated oven and cook for 20 to 25 minutes, until the chicken goujons are golden brown and cooked through. They should be white in the middle, with no pink. (Read the tips on page 10 about how to check that the chicken is cooked.)

9. Serve the crispy chicken goujons with the secret sauce on the side for dipping.

OVEN-BAKED BBQ CHICKEN WINGS

These wings taste great on their own with just the spice mix, but they're even better (and messier!) with a squirt of barbecue sauce. We've given you a recipe for a homemade barbecue spice mix here, but to make this even easier, you could use 3 tablespoons of a shop-bought barbecue seasoning instead. Get the napkins ready!

Serves 4

800g chicken wings

2 tablespoons olive oil

For the barbecue spice mix:

1 tablespoon light brown sugar

1 teaspoon smoked paprika

1 teaspoon paprika

1 teaspoon garlic powder

1 teaspoon onion powder

1 teaspoon dried oregano

1 teaspoon salt

1 teaspoon ground white pepper

a pinch of cayenne pepper (optional)

To serve (optional):

2 tablespoons barbecue sauce

To garnish:

4 fresh chives

1. Preheat your oven to 200°C for a conventional oven or 180°C for a fan oven.
2. Line a large baking tray with non-stick baking paper, then put a wire cooling rack on top of the lined tray.
3. To make the spice mix, put all the ingredients in a large bowl and mix together.
4. Pat the wings dry with kitchen paper, then put them in the bowl with the spice mix. Patting them dry first removes moisture, which helps them cook better. Drizzle the oil over the wings, then use your hands to toss them around, making sure they're all coated in the spice mix and oil.
5. Put the wings on the wire rack in a single layer.
6. Put the tray in the preheated oven and cook for 25 minutes. Use oven gloves to carefully remove the tray from the oven and put it on a wooden chopping board or on the hob to protect your countertop. Turn over each wing using kitchen tongs, then put the tray back in the oven and cook for 25 minutes more, until the wings are crispy.
7. These wings are great just like this, but we love to up the flavour game by putting them in a bowl, adding 2 tablespoons of barbecue sauce and stirring until they're all coated, then serving them sticky.
8. Use clean kitchen scissors to snip the chives into small pieces. Put the wings on a large plate and scatter over the chives. Don't forget the napkins!

CHICKEN SATAY SKEWERS

Food on a stick just tastes better, doesn't it? These simple chicken satay skewers are easy enough for a weeknight dinner, but good enough for special occasions too.

Makes 12

4 chicken fillets

1 tablespoon sesame oil

salt and pepper

12 bamboo skewers

For the satay sauce:

1 onion

2 garlic cloves

a thumb-sized piece of fresh ginger

1 tablespoon sesame oil

2 tablespoons medium curry powder

150ml water

3 tablespoons crunchy peanut butter

3 tablespoons sweet chilli sauce

1 tablespoon soy sauce

To garnish:

a few sprigs of fresh coriander

1. Preheat your oven to 200°C for a conventional oven or 180°C for a fan oven.

2. Line a baking tray with non-stick baking paper.

3. Tear off two more large pieces of non-stick baking paper. Put one piece of paper on a large chopping board and put a chicken fillet on top. Cover it with the second sheet of paper, then give the chicken a good bash with a rolling pin or meat tenderiser (the thing that looks like a hammer) to flatten it. Try to make sure it's an even thickness all over. This helps it cook faster (and it's pretty fun too). Put the flattened chicken on a plate, then bash the other fillets the same way.

4. Using clean kitchen scissors, cut the flattened chicken into strips, then put them in a mixing bowl. Drizzle the sesame oil over the chicken and add a little salt and pepper. Use your clean hands to toss together to coat all the chicken in the oil.

5. Thread the chicken strips onto your skewers (skewer time = fun time!). To do this, take one end of a chicken strip and carefully pierce it onto a skewer, then weave it in and out to create an S, leaving a small space at the bottom as a handle to hold. Put the skewers on the lined baking tray in a single layer.

6. Put the tray in the preheated oven and cook for 20 to 25 minutes, until the chicken is fully cooked – it should be white in the middle, with no pink. (Read the tips on page 10 about how to check that the chicken is cooked.)

7. While the chicken cooks, make the satay sauce. Peel and chop the onion. Peel and grate the garlic and ginger.

8. Pour the sesame oil into a saucepan, then put the pan on a medium heat on the hob. Let the oil warm up for a few minutes, then add the onion and cook for 5 minutes, until it's soft and golden. Add the garlic and ginger and cook for 1 minute. Stir in the curry powder and let it cook for 1 minute – your kitchen will smell amazing by now!

9. Add the water, then stir in the peanut butter, sweet chilli sauce and soy sauce. Let it simmer for 1 minute. If it's too thick, add a little more water until it's just right.

10 Use oven gloves to carefully remove the tray from the oven and put it on a wooden chopping board or on the hob to protect your countertop. Drizzle most of the satay sauce over the chicken skewers, turning to coat them in the sauce, then put the skewers on a nice serving plate.

11 Use clean kitchen scissors to snip the coriander into small pieces, then scatter it over the skewers to garnish. Pour the rest of the satay sauce into a bowl and put it on the side for dipping.

OUR KINDA FAMOUS CHICKEN CURRY

Once you see how easy it is to make a homemade curry paste, you'll never want to go back to store-bought jars. Plus our curry is kinda famous – we've even cooked it on the telly!

Serves 4

1 medium white onion
1 garlic clove
1 red pepper
4 chicken fillets
1 tablespoon vegetable oil
50ml water
1 x 400ml tin of coconut milk or 300ml cream

For the curry paste:

2 tablespoons medium curry powder
2 tablespoons tomato purée
1 tablespoon mango chutney
1 teaspoon mixed spice
1 teaspoon ground turmeric
1 teaspoon ground cumin

To serve:

perfect boiled rice (page 30)

To garnish:

fresh coriander or parsley leaves

1. Peel the onion, then cut it into slices. Peel and grate the garlic. Slice the red pepper. Use clean kitchen scissors to cut the chicken fillets into strips.

2. To make the homemade curry paste, put the curry powder, tomato purée, mango chutney, mixed spice, turmeric and cumin in a small bowl and mix together.

3. Put the oil in a saucepan, then put the pan on a medium heat on the hob. Let the oil warm up for a few minutes, then add the onion and garlic and cook 1 minute to give them a head start. Add the red pepper and chicken strips, then add the curry paste and the water and stir together. Cook for 5 minutes. It will smell amazing.

4. Pour in the coconut milk or cream and cover the pan with a lid. Turn the heat down to low and simmer for 20 minutes, until the chicken is cooked (read the tips on page 10 about how to check that the chicken is cooked).

5. Cook the rice using the recipe on page 30 while the curry simmers.

6. Serve the curry with the perfect boiled rice. To garnish, scatter over a few fresh coriander or parsley leaves.

LILS'S SPAGHETTI BOLOGNESE

I have a confession: I have cooking disasters all the time. One of the biggest happened just before a cooking class. I was trying out the spaghetti twist trick that we talk about on page 42 while Mum was busy setting everything up. Well, the whole saucepan with all the spaghetti fell straight onto the floor.

Meanwhile, a bunch of kids were already waiting in the Zoom class, so we quickly scooped up all the spaghetti, threw it back in the saucepan and started the class. I told everyone what had just happened, and the kids thought it was hilarious. (For the record, I nailed the spaghetti twist trick perfectly during the class.)

Here's a top tip: you can transform leftover Bolognese into a chilli con carne for a different dinner to use as a topping for a crispy-skin baked potato (page 41) or to serve with perfect boiled rice (page 30).

Serves 4

1 onion

1 carrot

1 red pepper

1 garlic clove

1 tablespoon olive oil

500g beef mince

salt and pepper

1 x 400g tin of whole plum tomatoes

2 tablespoons tomato purée

1 tablespoon dried oregano

1 bunch of fresh basil

1 chicken stock pot

1. Peel the onion and carrot, then chop them into small pieces. Cut the red pepper into small pieces. Peel and grate the garlic.

2. Put the oil in a large heavy-based saucepan, then put the pan on a medium heat on the hob. Let the oil warm up for a few minutes, then add the onion, carrot, red pepper and garlic to the pan and stir to coat them in the oil. Cook for about 5 minutes, until the veggies start to get soft.

3. Add the beef mince to the pan with a big pinch of salt and pepper. Use a wooden spoon to break up any big clumps of beef, then mix the beef and seasoning into the veggies. Cook for 5 to 7 minutes, until the mince is brown all over.

4. Stir in the tinned tomatoes, tomato purée and oregano. Use a wooden spoon to break up the whole tomatoes. Tear the basil leaves off the stems. Save a few for garnish at the end, then use your hands to tear the rest of the leaves into small pieces and add them to the pan. Let it simmer for 1 minute, then drop in the chicken stock pot.

5. Grate the Parmesan, then stir half of the cheese into the sauce. Put a lid on the pan and turn the heat down to very low. Let the sauce simmer while you cook the spaghetti.

50g Parmesan cheese

400g spaghetti

To serve:

cheesy garlic flatbread (page 142)

6   Put the spaghetti in a large pot and give it a twist in the middle with both hands. This simple trick helps prevent the spaghetti from sticking to the bottom of the pot (but fair warning, this was the twist that landed the spaghetti on the floor during one of our classes!). Now cook the pasta using the method on page 43.

7   When the spaghetti is ready, drain it in a colander in the sink.

8   The rule for spag Bol is to always add the pasta to the sauce, not the other way around! So using kitchen tongs, add the drained spaghetti to the pan, tossing to coat it all in the sauce.

9   To serve, divide the spag Bol among four pasta bowls. Sprinkle with the rest of the grated Parmesan and tear over the basil leaves that you saved earlier. Do I even need to say that this is so good served with cheesy garlic flatbread?

FISH TACO PARTY

We love a taco party on a Saturday night. The kitchen is buzzing with good vibes, from setting up the breading station to setting the table for the feast. It's the kind of meal where everyone can dive in, build their own tacos and enjoy some great chats. It's what Saturdays are all about: food, family and fun.

Serves 4

4 x 125g white fish fillets, such as cod, hake or haddock, skinned and boned (ask the fishmonger to do this for you or you can buy pre-packed fillets from the fridge section in the supermarket)

100g plain flour

salt and pepper

2 eggs

100g panko breadcrumbs

1 teaspoon smoked paprika

1 teaspoon ground cumin

1 teaspoon garlic powder

1 teaspoon onion powder

½ teaspoon chilli powder

1. Preheat your oven to 200°C for a conventional oven or 180°C for a fan oven.

2. Line a baking tray with non-stick baking paper.

3. First make the salsa using the recipe on page 144.

4. Using clean kitchen scissors, cut the fish fillets into strips. As you're cutting them, feel for any bones that might be hiding. If you find any, they are usually lined up in a strip, so you can just cut out that strip.

5. To set up your breading station, you need three bowls. Put the flour and a little salt and pepper in one bowl and mix together. Crack the eggs into the second bowl, then whisk with a fork. Put the breadcrumbs, smoked paprika, cumin, garlic powder, onion powder and chilli powder in the third bowl and mix together. Line them up in a row: flour first, then eggs, then breadcrumbs.

6. Dip each piece of fish into the flour first, then the eggs, then the breadcrumbs, making sure it's completely coated in breadcrumbs. Put the breaded fish on the lined baking tray in a single layer.

7. Put the tray in the preheated oven and bake for 15 to 20 minutes, until the fish is golden and crispy.

8. To warm the tortillas, tear off a large sheet of foil. Stack the tortillas on top of each other, then wrap them in the foil. Put them on the lower shelf of the oven during the last 5 minutes of the cooking time for the fish.

9. While the fish is cooking, shred the lettuce using the scatter method on page 23. Cut the lime into wedges. Grate the Cheddar. Put the lettuce, lime wedges, cheese and salsa in separate bowls and set them on the table.

10. Using oven gloves, carefully remove the tray from the oven and put it on a wooden chopping board or on the hob to protect your countertop. Remove the foil-wrapped tortillas too.

To serve:

salsa (page 144)

8 corn tortillas

½ head of iceberg lettuce

1 lime

100g mature Cheddar cheese

11 Use tongs to put the crispy fish on a serving plate. Unwrap the tortillas and put them on a separate plate.

12 Bring the fish and tortillas to the table to let everyone build their own tacos and dig in.

SW
TRE

EE T
ATS

CHOCOLATE-COVERED COCONUT BARS

Did you know that a coconut is actually a fruit? I always thought it was a giant nut!

These coconut bars will transport you to a tropical paradise with just three ingredients. And unlike the bars in the shops, you can make these as big as your heart desires.

Makes 8 to 10

250g desiccated coconut, plus extra to decorate

1 x 375g tin of condensed milk

300g milk chocolate, plus extra to decorate

1. Line a baking tray with non-stick baking paper.

2. Put the coconut and condensed milk in a large mixing bowl and stir together. It will be very thick.

3. Run your hands under the tap – damp hands make it easier to work with the sticky mixture. Form the mixture into eight or 10 oval-shaped bars and put them on the lined baking tray. Put the tray in the fridge for at least 4 hours to let the bars firm up.

4. When the bars are firm, break the chocolate into squares and put the pieces in a heatproof bowl that will sit snugly on top of a saucepan.

5. Fill the saucepan only one-quarter full of water. Put the pan on a medium heat on the hob. Wait until the water is simmering, then put the bowl on top of the pan, making sure the water doesn't touch the bottom of the bowl or it will ruin the chocolate and make it grainy. Stir now and then, until the chocolate has completely melted. Carefully take the bowl off the top of the pan, but watch out for steam. Put the bowl on a potholder, a wooden chopping board or on the hob to protect your countertop.

6. Lower each coconut bar into the melted chocolate, making sure it's fully coated. Use two forks to remove each bar. Put the chocolate-covered bars back on the lined baking tray, then put the tray back in the fridge for about 3 hours, until the chocolate has set.

7. If you like, you can melt some extra chocolate the same way you did in step 5, then use a spoon to drizzle it over the top of the set bars and sprinkle them with a little more coconut.

8. Store the bars in an airtight container in the fridge for up to four days.

ROCKY ROAD ADVENTURE BARS

I'm the adventurer in the family, and I love a good roller coaster. This rocky road is like throwing popcorn, marshmallows, biscuits and chocolate onto the Cú Chulainn roller coaster at Emerald Park, twisting, turning and crunching it all together. Each crunchy, chewy, chocolatey bite is full of surprises.

Makes 12

400g milk chocolate

120g unsalted butter

100g golden syrup

120g Maltesers

120g Crunchie bars

100g bourbon biscuits

80g mini marshmallows

60g cooked popcorn

1. Line a 33cm x 23cm rectangular tin with enough non-stick baking paper that it comes up over the sides a little (read page 6 for tips on how to line a rectangular baking tin).

2. Break the chocolate into squares, then put it in a heatproof bowl with the butter and golden syrup.

3. Fill a saucepan only one-quarter full of water. Put the pan on a medium heat on the hob. Wait until the water is simmering, then put the bowl on top of the pan, making sure the water doesn't touch the bottom of the bowl or it will ruin the chocolate and make it grainy. Let the chocolate, butter and golden syrup all melt together, stirring now and then until it's smooth. Turn off the heat, then put the bowl on a potholder or wooden chopping board.

4. Put the Maltesers, Crunchie bars and bourbon biscuits in a ziplock bag and seal it closed. Gently bash them with a rolling pin to break them into chunks. Tip them into the bowl with the melted chocolate.

5. Add the marshmallows and popcorn to the bowl, then stir gently until everything is coated with melted chocolate.

6. Scoop the mixture into the lined tin, then use the back of a spoon to press it down firmly into an even layer. Let it cool, then put the tin in the fridge for at least 4 hours to harden.

7. When it's firm, use the paper to lift the slab of rocky road onto a chopping board. Cut into 12 bars. Store the bars in an airtight container in the fridge for up to four days for an anytime adventure snack.

EASY CARAMEL SQUARES

These easy caramel squares are just as good as your favourite café treat. They're perfect for sharing ... or not!

Makes 12

100g unsalted butter

300g digestive biscuits

1 x 400g tin of caramel

300g milk chocolate

1. Line a 20cm square baking tin with enough non-stick baking paper that it comes up over the sides a little (read page 6 for tips on how to line a square baking tin).

2. Put the butter in a small saucepan, then put the pan on a medium heat on the hob. Let the butter melt, then turn off the heat and let it cool a little.

3. Put the digestives in a ziplock bag and seal it closed, then gently bash them with a rolling pin to break them into fine crumbs.

4. Pour the biscuit crumbs into the saucepan, then stir them into the melted butter.

5. Tip the crumbs into the lined baking tin. Use your hands to firmly pat the crumbs down into an even layer, making sure you get them into the corners too. Put the tin in the fridge for 1 hour to let the biscuit base firm up.

6. Spoon the tinned caramel over the biscuit base, then spread it evenly with the back of the spoon. Pop the tin back in the fridge and let the caramel set for at least 2 hours.

7. Break the chocolate into squares. If you have a microwave, put the chocolate pieces in a small bowl and microwave for 30 seconds at a time, checking until it's all melted.

8. If you don't have a microwave, fill a saucepan only one-quarter full of water, then put the pan on a medium heat on the hob. Wait until the water is simmering, then put the chocolate pieces in a heatproof bowl that sits snugly on top of the saucepan, making sure the water doesn't touch the bottom of the bowl or it will ruin the chocolate and make it grainy. Stir now and then, until the chocolate has completely melted. Take the bowl off the top of the pan, but watch out for steam.

9. Pour the melted chocolate over the set caramel and spread it out smoothly with the back of a spoon. Put the tin back in the fridge overnight to fully set.

10. The next day, use the baking paper to lift the slab out of the tin and onto a chopping board, then cut into 12 small squares. Don't worry if the chocolate cracks when you cut the slab, it happens! Store the squares in an airtight container in the fridge for up to four days.

NO-BAKE STRAWBERRY CHEESECAKE CUPS

Last year I decided to go for a no-bake strawberry cheesecake instead of a traditional birthday cake, and it was the best choice ever. This is basically an assembly job, no oven needed.

Makes 4

60g salted butter
100g digestive biscuits
340g cream cheese
60g icing sugar
1 teaspoon vanilla extract
100g fresh strawberries, plus extra to decorate
60g strawberry jam
1 tablespoon water

To decorate:

squirty cream

1. Put the butter in a small saucepan, then put the pan on a medium heat on the hob. Let the butter melt, then turn off the heat and let it cool a little.

2. Put the digestives in a ziplock bag and seal it closed, then gently bash them with a rolling pin to break them into fine crumbs.

3. Pour the biscuit crumbs into the saucepan and stir them into the melted butter. Divide the mixture evenly among four small cups or ramekins. Press it down firmly to form the base.

4. Put the cream cheese, icing sugar and vanilla in a mixing bowl and stir together until smooth and creamy.

5. Chop the strawberries using the scatter method on page 23.

6. Gently stir in the chopped strawberries. Try not to crush them, otherwise the mixture will be too wet.

7. Put the strawberry jam in a small bowl, then stir in the tablespoon of water to make it slightly more pourable. Spoon a thin layer of jam over the cookie crust in each cup.

8. Spoon the cream cheese and strawberry mixture on top of the jam layer in the cups. Smooth the tops with the back of the spoon.

9. Top with squirty cream and decorate with a few fresh strawberry slices.

HOMEMADE ICE CREAM

Keep the summertime vibes alive all year round with the easiest, creamiest homemade ice cream. You can swirl in your favourite jam, caramel, chocolate spread or fruit coulis. Or you can add all sorts of mix-ins, like chopped nuts, mini marshmallows, Smarties, broken-up biscuits or chopped-up leftover Halloween or Easter candy. It's a perfect match for lots of the treats in this chapter or simply piled high in a cone. And the best part? No ice cream machine needed.

Serves 10

500ml double cream

200g condensed milk

2 teaspoons vanilla extract

your favourite mix-ins (see the intro)

1. Pour the cream into a large bowl. Using an electric mixer, whip the cream just until it makes soft peaks. When you lift the beaters out of the cream, look at the tip of the whipped cream. If it stands up like little mountain peaks and droops over at the tip, that's the perfect soft peak stage.

2. Pour in the condensed milk and vanilla, then beat until soft peaks form again.

3. Here's your chance to get creative. Add a swirl of caramel, chocolate spread or even cocoa powder. For a fruity twist, try mixing through some jam or a berry coulis for a raspberry or strawberry ripple.

4. Pour the ice cream mixture into a 2-pound loaf tin, cover the top tightly with cling film and pop it in the freezer. Now comes the hard part: waiting until it freezes solid. This should take 3 or 4 hours or you can leave it overnight.

5. Now you've got rich, creamy ice cream, ready to scoop and enjoy.

TRADITIONAL SPONGE TRAY BAKE

This classic cake is perfect for birthdays, bake sales or any special occasion – or just because! The foolproof all-in-one method (which is another way of saying stirring everything together in one bowl) saves time and washing-up and makes a light, fluffy sponge.

Makes 9 squares

200g unsalted butter

200g self-raising flour

200g caster sugar

3 eggs

1 teaspoon baking powder

2 teaspoons vanilla extract

For the icing:

200g icing sugar

3 to 4 teaspoons water (just enough to form a thick icing)

To decorate:

a handful of coloured sprinkles

1. Take the butter out of the fridge, put it in a large bowl and let it sit on the countertop for at least 30 minutes to let it get soft.

2. Meanwhile, preheat your oven to 200°C for a conventional oven or 180°C for a fan oven.

3. Line a 20cm square baking tin with non-stick baking paper (read page 6 for tips on how to line a square baking tin).

4. You're going to make the cake batter using the all-in-one method, so put the flour, sugar, eggs, baking powder and vanilla in the bowl with the soft butter. Mix everything together using a wooden spoon or an electric mixer until smooth.

5. Scoop the batter into the lined baking tin, spreading it evenly into the corners.

6. Put the tin in the preheated oven and bake for 40 minutes.

7. Using oven gloves, carefully remove the tin from the oven and put it on a wooden chopping board or on the hob to protect your countertop. To test if the cake is done, insert a skewer, cake tester or small knife into the middle of the cake. If it comes out clean, with no batter sticking to it, the cake is done, so use your oven gloves again to move it to a wire cooling rack. If the tester doesn't come out clean, put the cake back in the oven for 5 more minutes and test it again.

8. Let the cake get completely cool on the wire rack.

9. To make the icing, sift the icing sugar into a large bowl by putting it in a large fine mesh sieve. Holding the handle of the sieve with one hand, and with the sieve raised up above the bowl, use your other hand to tap the side of the sieve so that the sugar gently falls into the bowl. Sifting the icing sugar means your icing won't have any lumps in it.

10 Add 3 teaspoons of water and whisk it into the icing sugar. You want a smooth, thick icing, but if it's too thick, add 1 more teaspoon of water.

11 When the cake has completely cooled, spread the icing evenly over the top. Decorate with lots of coloured sprinkles.

12 Let the icing harden, then cut the cake into nine squares.

SWEET TREATS

NUTTY BISCOFF PINWHEELS

You'll go nuts for these nutty Biscoff pinwheels. They are so easy to make but they taste like they came from the bakery. With flaky puff pastry, creamy Biscoff spread and crunchy nuts, they're the perfect mix of sweet and nutty – just like my friends!

Makes 10

a little plain flour, for dusting your countertop

1 sheet of ready-rolled puff pastry

150g Biscoff spread (or you could use Nutella or peanut butter)

100g chopped walnuts

1 egg

For the icing:

120g icing sugar

2 to 3 tablespoons milk

½ teaspoon vanilla extract

1. If your pastry is frozen, put it in the fridge overnight to thaw it.

2. The next day, preheat your oven to 200°C for a conventional oven or 180°C for a fan oven.

3. Line a baking tray with non-stick baking paper.

4. Sprinkle a little flour on your clean countertop, then unroll the sheet of puff pastry on it.

5. Spread the Biscoff evenly over the pastry, leaving a space clear at one short edge. Sprinkle most of the chopped nuts over the Biscoff layer.

6. Roll up the pastry into a tight log, then cut it into slices 2.5cm thick to make the pinwheels. Put the pinwheels on the lined baking tray, cut side up so that you can see the Biscoff swirl.

7. Crack the egg into a small bowl, then whisk with a fork. Use a pastry brush to paint the tops and sides of the pinwheels with the beaten egg for a golden finish.

8. Put the tray in the preheated oven and bake for 15 to 20 minutes, until the pinwheels are golden and puffed up.

9. Using oven gloves, carefully remove the tray from the oven and put it on a wire cooling rack. Let the pinwheels cool a little while you make the icing.

10. Put the icing sugar, 2 tablespoons of milk and the vanilla in a small bowl and whisk until it's smooth. If the icing is too thick, add another tablespoon of milk.

11. Using a spoon, drizzle the icing over the slightly cooled pinwheels, then sprinkle with the rest of the nuts for extra crunch.

COOKIE CROISSANTS

Also known as Le Crookie, my mum first spotted these on YouTube Shorts when they went viral (even though, you know, she totally doesn't watch YouTube). She showed them to me, and let me tell you, they looked so good I was practically licking the screen. You won't be able to resist the warm, flaky croissant combined with the gooey, sweet cookie filling.

We've given you a recipe for homemade cookie dough, but you could use shop-bought cookie dough to make these even easier.

Makes 4

50g cold salted butter

50g light brown sugar

50g caster sugar

1 egg

1 teaspoon vanilla extract

130g plain flour

4 croissants (stale ones work too)

To drizzle:

shop-bought chocolate or caramel sauce

1 tablespoon icing sugar

To serve (optional):

homemade ice cream (page 170)

1. Preheat your oven to 200°C for a conventional oven or 180°C for a fan oven.

2. Line a baking tray with non-stick baking paper.

3. To make the cookie dough, grate the cold butter into a large mixing bowl using the large holes on a box grater. Add the light brown sugar and caster sugar and beat together with a wooden spoon.

4. Crack the egg into the bowl, then add the vanilla and mix again.

5. Add the flour, then gently stir until you have a smooth cookie dough.

6. To prepare your croissants, lay them flat on your chopping board and put your hand on top to steady it. Use a serrated bread knife in a gentle sawing motion to cut each one horizontally through the centre, but not all the way through – you want to create a pocket for the cookie dough in the middle.

7. Stuff the inside of each croissant with a generous amount of cookie dough. Put a little extra cookie dough on top of each croissant for maximum cookie goodness. Put the stuffed croissants on the lined baking tray.

8. Put the tray in the preheated oven and bake for 20 minutes, until the cookie dough is golden and baked through.

9. Using oven gloves, carefully remove the tray from the oven and put it on a wire cooling rack. Let the crookies cool for a few minutes.

10. Drizzle the crookies with some shop-bought chocolate or caramel sauce. Put the icing sugar in a small fine mesh sieve, then hold it over the croissants and gently tap the side to sift the sugar over the croissants to give them a light dusting.

11. Try this with a scoop of homemade ice cream for an even more indulgent treat.

COSY APPLE CRUMBLE

As soon as we go back to school after the summer break, I start counting down to cosy apple crumble nights. These happen on Friday evenings, when we eat our crumble in the sitting room with the fire blazing, trying our best not to spill crumbs on the couch – even though my dog, Noodles, is always ready and waiting to hoover them up!

Serves 4

4 large Bramley cooking apples

2 tablespoons light brown sugar

1 teaspoon ground cinnamon

½ teaspoon ground ginger

For the crumble:

160g plain flour

100g cold salted butter

100g caster sugar

For the topping:

2 tablespoons porridge oats

2 tablespoons light brown sugar

To serve:

homemade ice cream (page 170)

1. Preheat your oven to 200°C for a conventional oven or 180°C for a fan oven.
2. Peel the apples, then cut them in half. Cut the halves into slices, then cut the slices into bite-sized pieces, making sure you avoid the seeds. Put the apple pieces in a baking dish and sprinkle with the brown sugar, cinnamon and ginger. Use your clean hands to toss everything together to coat the apples in the sugar and spices.
3. Put the flour in a large mixing bowl. Grate the cold butter into the flour using the large holes of a box grater. Rub the butter and flour together with your fingertips until the mixture looks like fine breadcrumbs. Add the caster sugar and rub that in too.
4. Put the oats and brown sugar in a separate small bowl and mix them together.
5. Sprinkle the crumble mixture evenly over the apples in the baking dish, then sprinkle over the oat topping for extra crunch.
6. Put the dish in the preheated oven and bake for 25 to 30 minutes, until the apples are soft and the crumble is golden and crunchy.
7. Using oven gloves, carefully remove the dish from the oven and put it on a wooden chopping board or on the hob to protect your countertop. Let the crumble cool for a few minutes.
8. To serve, divide the crumble among four bowls. Add a scoop of homemade ice cream to each bowl and eat while the crumble is still warm.

BUTTERFLY BUNS

Mum says these are such a classic recipe that they just had to be in the book. I say they're the perfect cupcakes, complete with wings. Did you know a group of butterflies is called a kaleidoscope of butterflies? So don't forget to use some pretty coloured bun cases to match!

Makes 12

1 tablespoon vegetable oil, if needed for greasing the tin

100g cold unsalted butter

120g self-raising flour

100g caster sugar

2 eggs

50g strawberry jam

For the buttercream icing:

100g unsalted butter

250g icing sugar

1 teaspoon vanilla extract

1. Preheat your oven to 200°C for a conventional oven or 180°C for a fan oven.

2. Line a 12-hole muffin tin with paper liners (or read page 6 to make your own bakery-style liners) or lightly grease each hole by putting a little oil on a piece of kitchen paper, then using the paper to rub the bottom and sides of each hole. Or if you have a silicone muffin tray, use that, but still be sure to grease the holes.

3. Grate the butter into a large mixing bowl using the large holes on a box grater. Add the flour and sugar and stir them all together. Crack the eggs into the bowl, then mix with a wooden spoon just until it's a smooth batter. Try not to overmix or your buns will be tough. Spoon 1 tablespoon of batter into each hole.

4. Put the muffin tin on a baking tray to make it easier to get it in and out of the oven, especially if you've used a silicone tray. Put the tin in the preheated oven and bake for 15 to 20 minutes, until the buns are golden brown. Using oven gloves, carefully remove the tin from the oven and put it on a wire cooling rack. Let the buns cool completely. If you put buttercream on them while they're still warm, it will melt.

5. To make the buttercream, take the butter out of the fridge and let it sit on the countertop for at least 30 minutes to get soft. Put the soft butter in a large bowl.

6. To sift the icing sugar into the bowl, put it in a large fine mesh sieve. Holding the handle of the sieve with one hand, and with the sieve raised up above the bowl, use your other hand to tap the side of the sieve so that the sugar falls into the bowl. Sifting the icing sugar means your buttercream won't have any lumps in it.

7. Add the vanilla to the bowl, then use an electric mixer to mix everything together until the icing is smooth and fluffy.

8. When the buns have cooled, use a butter knife to cut a small piece out of the centre top of each bun. Cut these pieces in half to create your butterfly wings.

9. Fill each hole with a teaspoon of jam and some buttercream. Put the butterfly wings back on top, then watch them fly into your mouth and disappear.

INDEX

A

apples
    apple and banana oat bakes 75
    cosy apple crumble 179
    five-a-day lunchbox muffins 76–7
    how to peel and grate 19
    pork and apple sausage rolls 88–9
    sausage and apple tray bake with sweet potato curls 131

B

bagels
    egg mayonnaise on toasted bagels 68–9
baking trays and tins, how to line 6
bananas
    apple and banana oat bakes 75
    five-a-day lunchbox muffins 76–7
barbecue
    oven-baked BBQ chicken wings 151
bars
    apple and banana oat bakes 75
    chocolate-covered coconut bars 163
    rocky road adventure bars 164
beans
    posh beans on toast 65
beef
    double cheese, double burger 134–5
    kofta tray bake 136–7
    Lils's spaghetti Bolognese 156–7
    meatball subs 104–5
    one-pot Swedish meatballs 132
berries
    tropical berry smoothie bowl 54
Biscoff
    nutty Biscoff pinwheels 175
blender, how to use 9
bridge method 22
buns
    butterfly buns 180
burgers
    double cheese, double burger 134–5
buttermilk
    flipping great buttermilk pancakes 60

C

cake
    traditional sponge tray bake 172–3
caramel
    easy caramel squares 166
carrots
    five-a-day lunchbox muffins 76–7
    how to make carrot ribbons 17
cheese
    20-minute feta and cherry tomato tagliatelle tray bake 119
    cheesy garlic flatbread 142–3
    double cheese, double burger 134–5
    epic ham and cheese toastie 70–1
    ham and cheese croissants 115
    how to grate 17
    jambons 86
    mini cheese scones 78–9
    movie night nachos 144–5
    speedy mac 'n' cheese 107
    tuna and sweetcorn melt 99

cheesecake
    no-bake strawberry cheesecake cups 169
chicken
    chicken fajita tray bake 120–1
    chicken satay skewers 152–3
    chopped chicken wrap 97
    crispy chicken goujons with secret sauce 149
    how to slice a chicken fillet 19
    how to test that chicken is cooked 10
    one-pot lemon pepper chicken drumsticks with rice 124–5
    our kinda famous chicken curry 154
    oven-baked BBQ chicken wings 151
    quick chicken ramen 103
    spice bag tray bake 122–3
chocolate
    chocolate-covered coconut bars 163
    easy caramel squares 166
    rocky road adventure bars 164
chopping boards 24–5
ciabattas
    tuna and sweetcorn melt 99
    turkey nugget ciabattas 85
cinnamon
    cinnamon French toast hugs 63
claw method 22
coconut
    chocolate-covered coconut bars 163
cookies
    cookie croissants 176

cream cheese
    no-bake strawberry cheesecake cups 169
    smoked salmon and cream cheese pinwheels 81
croissants
    cookie croissants 177
    ham and cheese croissants 115
crumble
    cosy apple crumble 179
curry
    our kinda famous chicken curry 154

D
dumplings, oven-baked 146–7

E
eggs
    cracking good egg-fried rice 32
    egg mayonnaise on toasted bagels 68–9
    how to crack 9
    jammy eggs and toast soldiers 57
    mini quiches 90–1
    sausage and egg muffins 66–7

F
fajitas
    chicken fajita tray bake 120–1
feta
    20-minute feta and cherry tomato tagliatelle tray bake 119
filo pastry
    crunchy prawn spring rolls 111
fish
    fancy fish 'n' chips 126–7
    fish taco party 158–9
    smoked salmon and cream cheese pinwheels 81
    sticky salmon tray bake 128–9
    tuna and sweetcorn melt 99
flatbread
    cheesy garlic flatbread 142–3
French toast
    cinnamon French toast hugs 63

G
garlic
    cheesy garlic flatbread 142–3
    how to peel and grate 14
ginger
    how to peel and grate 14
goujons
    crispy chicken goujons with secret sauce 149
guacamole
    movie night nachos 144–5

H
ham
    epic ham and cheese toastie 70–1
    ham and cheese croissants 115
    jambons 86
herbs, how to chop 19
hob, how to use 9
hot food
    how to drain 10
    how to remove from the oven 10

I
ice cream
    homemade ice cream 170

J
jambons 86

K
kitchen hygiene 24–5
kitchen rules 26
knives
    how to clean 20
    safety tips 20

L
lamb
    kofta tray bake 136–7

M
meatballs
    kofta tray bake 136–7
    meatball subs 104–5
    one-pot Swedish meatballs 132
mezzaluna 23
muffin liners, how to make 6
muffins
    five-a-day lunchbox muffins 76–7
    sausage and egg muffins 66–7

N
nachos
    movie night nachos 144–5
noodles
    quick chicken ramen 103
    sticky salmon tray bake 128–9
nuggets
    turkey nugget ciabattas 85

O
oats
    apple and banana oat bakes 75
    crunchy granola 53
one-pot wonders
    one-pot lemon pepper chicken drumsticks with rice 124–5
    one-pot Swedish meatballs 132
onion goggles 17
onions, how to chop 17
oven, how to preheat 4

P
pancakes
    flipping great buttermilk pancakes 60
pasta
    20-minute feta and cherry tomato tagliatelle tray bake 119
    creamy, crunchy pasta salad 92
    how to cook 43
    Lils's spaghetti Bolognese 156–7
    shapes 42
    spaghetti aglio e olio 45
    spaghetti carbonara 108
    speedy mac 'n' cheese 107
pepper, how to season food with 9
peppers, how to slice or dice 17
pesto
    pesto rosso 82
pinwheels
    nutty Biscoff pinwheels 175
    smoked salmon and cream cheese pinwheels 81
pizza 140–1
    four-fold pizza wraps 100

pork
    double cheese, double burger 134–5
    oven-baked dumplings 146–7
    pork and apple sausage rolls 88–9
    sausage and apple tray bake with sweet potato curls 131
    sausage and egg muffins 66–7
potatoes
    crispy-skin baked potatoes 38–9
    jacket potato toppings 41
    oven-baked gnocchi 36–7
    perfect mashed potatoes 34–5
    sausage and apple tray bake with sweet potato curls 131
prawns
    crunchy prawn spring rolls 111
puff pastry
    ham and cheese croissants 115
    jambons 86
    nutty Biscoff pinwheels 175
    pork and apple sausage rolls 88–9

R
ramen
    quick chicken ramen 103
raspberries
    enormous raspberry scones 58–9
rice
    cracking good egg-fried rice 32
    golden veggie rice 112
    one-pot lemon pepper chicken drumsticks with rice 124–5
    one-pot Swedish meatballs 132
    perfect boiled white rice 30–1

S

salads
- creamy, crunchy pasta salad 92

salmon
- smoked salmon and cream cheese pinwheels 81
- sticky salmon tray bake 128–9

salsa
- movie night nachos 144–5

salt, how to season food with 9

satay
- chicken satay skewers 152–3

sauces
- arrabbiata sauce 48
- burger sauce 134–5
- classic tomato sauce 46
- cheese sauce 144–5
- crispy chicken goujons with secret sauce 149
- pesto rosso 82
- satay sauce 152–3
- tartar sauce 126–7

sausages
- pork and apple sausage rolls 88–9
- sausage and apple tray bake with sweet potato curls 131
- sausage and egg muffins 66–7

scatter method 23

scones
- enormous raspberry scones 58–9
- mini cheese scones 78–9

skewers
- chicken satay skewers 152–3

smoothie
- tropical berry smoothie bowl 54

spice bag tray bake 122–3

spring onions, how to prepare 17

spring rolls
- crunchy prawn spring rolls 111

strawberries
- no-bake strawberry cheesecake cups 169

subs
- meatball subs 104–5

sweet potatoes
- sausage and apple tray bake with sweet potato curls 131

sweetcorn
- tuna and sweetcorn melt 99

T

tacos
- fish taco party 158–9

toast
- jammy eggs and toast soldiers 57
- posh beans on toast 65

tomatoes
- 20-minute feta and cherry tomato tagliatelle tray bake 119
- arrabbiata sauce 48
- classic tomato sauce 46
- pesto rosso 82

tray bakes
- 20-minute feta and cherry tomato tagliatelle tray bake 119
- chicken fajita tray bake 120–1
- double cheese, double burger 134–5
- fancy fish 'n' chips 126–7
- kofta tray bake 136–7
- sausage and apple tray bake with sweet potato curls 131
- spice bag tray bake 122–3
- sticky salmon tray bake 128–9
- traditional sponge tray bake 172–3

tuna
- tuna and sweetcorn melt 99

turkey
- turkey nugget ciabattas 85

W

weighing ingredients 4

wraps
- chopped chicken wrap 97
- four-fold pizza wraps 100

Z

zesting 19

ACKNOWLEDGEMENTS

This book has been bursting to get out into the world for a long time. Lils and I dreamed of creating a cookbook for kids that wouldn't talk down to them, one that they would use with pride, that would grow with them and that they'd use for life.

From our very first meeting with Kristin Jensen, our publisher, she just got it and welcomed us into her incredible crew of experts and fellow cookbook authors at Nine Bean Rows and Blasta Books. Not only did they inspire me, they also inspired Lils in ways I never imagined. So thank you to our designer, Matt Cox (no relation, but go Team Cox!), our photographer, Clare Wilkinson, our stylist, Charlotte O'Connell, and assistants Safiq Murray and Susan Willis. You all believed in her and truly listened to her, never treating her as just a child. You showed her that she belongs in a room of incredibly talented people, even on days when I felt a bit out of my depth!

Thank you to all our family and friends who surround us with love and support.

A heartfelt mention to Daire, always our biggest supporter. Up Fermanagh!

Thank you to all the mothers, fathers, guardians, grandparents, sisters, brothers, sons, daughters and our furry family members (our non-battery-powered hoovers!) who have encouraged kids to cook.

A huge shoutout to all the amazing kids who cook with us every week as members of our cooking club. You inspire us more than you know with your creativity and passion in the kitchen. Your photos at the end of each class always bring a smile to our faces, and your constant support and encouragement remind us that we're on the right track. Keep cooking, keep smiling and keep inspiring!

A special thank you to Damien and Noodles the dog – one for following us around the kitchen, licking their lips, and the other for all their love and support (you know which one is which!).

And for Lils, my partner in this adventure, I am so lucky to do this with you. Watching you grow, dream big and work hard has been the greatest reward as a mother.

Jolene x

Nine Bean Rows
23 Mountjoy Square
Dublin, D01 E0F8
Ireland
@9beanrowsbooks
ninebeanrowsbooks.com

First published 2025
Text copyright © Jolene Cox and Lily Mae Cox, 2025
Photography copyright © Clare Wilkinson

ISBN: 978-1-7384795-4-2

Editor: Kristin Jensen
Photographer: Clare Wilkinson thymestudios.ie
Stylist: Charlotte O'Connell charlotteoconnell.co.uk
Assistants: Safiq Murray and Susan Willis
Designer: Matt Cox newmanandeastwood.com
Printed by L&C Printing Group, Poland

This product is made of material from well-managed FSC®-certified forests and other controlled sources.

All rights reserved.
No part of this publication may be copied, reproduced or transmitted in any form or by any means without written permission of the publishers.
A CIP catalogue record for this book is available from the British Library.
For EU product safety concerns, contact us at info@ninebeanrowsbooks.com.
10 9 8 7 6 5 4 3 2 1